REFASHIONED

CUTTING-EDGE CLOTHING
FROM UPCYCLED MATERIALS

SASS BROWN

Laurence King Publishing

LAURENCE KING

Published in 2013 by
Laurence King Publishing Ltd
361–373 City Road
London EC1V 1LR
United Kingdom
email: enquiries@laurenceking.com
www.laurenceking.com

Published in 2013 by
Laurence King Publishing Ltd

A catalogue record for this book
is available from the British Library

ISBN: 978 1 78067 301 1

Design by & SMITH

Printed in China

MIX
Paper from
responsible sources
FSC® C008047
FSC
www.fsc.org

Front cover (clockwise from top left):
Juana Díaz; Silent People; Hibrida; Jeffrey Wang;
Schmidt Takahashi; Trash-Couture; Tamara Fogle;
MAYER Peace Collection; Steinwidder; Artemas
Quibble and the Creatures of Mme du Barry
Back cover (clockwise from top left):
Atelier Awash; KONDAKIS; Rachel Freire;
Otra; Ute Decker; km/a; R.ds

Frontispiece: The BEA Project is an
exploration of fashion and art in mixed media,
which aims to dismantle existing perceptions
through deconstruction.

To Rosie on your 16th birthday!
Lots of love
Emma
xo.

REFASHIONED

CONTENTS

FOREWORD

ALABAMA CHANIN'S CELEBRATION OF
CRAFTSMANSHIP AND ARTISANSHIP IN
EVERYDAY LIFE EXTENDS THROUGHOUT
THE EXQUISITE COLLECTION, WHICH
HONOURS THE CREATOR IN US ALL.

During my years of working in the fashion industry, I have seen first-hand the effects of newer, faster and 'better' ways of living and buying. Ultimately, choosing faster and cheaper can equate to unwitting disregard for humanity and the environment.

It is often much easier to consume what is convenient without thinking too much about the larger impact or consequences of our choices – particularly the continuing use of toxic chemicals, haphazard disposal of these wastes, unprotected workers and unsafe practices. These conditions simply cannot be sustained long-term if we are to continue living on this beautiful blue planet. As globalization makes our fashion production more and more transparent, we are no longer blind to manufacturing methods. As the processes become understood by the end consumer, customers begin to make different choices. Patti Smith once said, 'I choose Earth'. I see a future where we all choose Earth.

I applaud the work of Sass Brown and all the designers and innovators who are working toward that future. I believe that the greater 'machine' can be slowed and reined in, and that beautiful ways of working can grow from that restraint. Those outlined in this book are individuals and companies that make me hopeful and are making a difference in the world today. For instance, the work of MAYER Peace Collection includes handcrafted tailored jackets and coordinating separates made from antique fabrics, and perfectly illustrates the beauty that comes from upcycling

material. Piece x Piece offers a personal response to the overwhelming amount of waste produced by the fashion industry by using waste cuttings from other garment producers. What would traditionally be considered trash and would find its way to a landfill is now the basis of stunning limited-edition pieces of clothing. As I read through Sass's book, I clearly see beautiful new values emerging on every front.

My journey with textiles spans my entire life, beginning with memories of my grandmother's sewing circles during humid summers in northern Alabama. The magnificent quilts made then are now considered valuable treasures, but were commonplace and practical at the time. These women 'upcycled' out of necessity, using fabric taken from salvaged flour sacks and outgrown Sunday dresses that had seen their last wearing. While these seamstresses surely never used the words upcycled, recycled or sustainable design, their common-sense approach and practicality are characteristics we should emulate and applaud.

My experience of over a decade with my company Alabama Chanin tells me that recycling and repurposing textiles lends to the complexity, artistry and value of a finished design. As people, our many roles change and evolve over the course of a lifetime; I love the idea that textiles can do the same. Sass Brown's work proves that reviving something in order for it to serve a new purpose can be a beautiful act of conservation, design and art.

Natalie Chanin,
Founder of Alabama Chanin

Rachel Freire

INTRODUCTION

This, my second book, is an outgrowth of my first – *Eco Fashion* – and in homage to the wealth of talented designers working with recycled and upcycled materials, who truly deserve their own book.

It showcases a range of gifted practitioners who use recycled and upcycled textiles, as well as clothing and hardware, to produce beautiful and desirable garments and accessories. I felt it was important to cover the gamut of intellectual, cerebral, avant-garde, cutting-edge, tongue-in-cheek and playful design in this book. Fashion and clothing play many roles in our lives, but unless they are well designed, they are simply not interesting. Theatrical, over the top, in your face: these are merely different provocations, but all worthy of our attention.

Fashion has power; at its best, it is inspirational and aspirational. In a world of simply too much stuff, it is vital that eco-fashion is not just good, is not just nice, but is in fact extraordinary. There is more than enough stuff in the world already – the idea of adding anything more that is not outstanding, seems unconscionable. If it is not exceptional, then it already exists; and no matter how ethical, organic or recycled the product is, it simply mimics or equals something already available, something that has already been produced, no matter how poorly. In terms of ecology, it is adding more stuff to a world already overburdened. Herein lies the value of recycled and upcycled

Above: Jeffrey Wang
Right: Raggedy

design: it employs materials that have already been produced, whether considered to have worth or not, whether already used or not. With 100,000 million tonnes of clothing thrown away each year in the UK alone, 50 per cent of which is destined for landfill,[1] the diversion and revaluing of those materials is no small task.

As a designer and writer, I like to tell the stories around our clothes, to help revive our material connection to our clothing. There is such a wealth of stories bursting for an audience, some ugly and painful, others beautiful and poetic. I strive to tell those stories through my work, promoting some truly amazing designers and artists en route, whose work deserves a greater audience as they make a difference in what they do as well as in how they do it. To that end, I consider myself a fashion activist. Why a fashion activist? Well, in a world where fast fashion is the norm, where most people purchase something to wear for a single evening that costs no more than a Chinese takeaway – and is thrown away as easily as the polystyrene container it comes in – investing in quality design, valuing traditional craft skills and purchasing ecologically sound design is, actually, a pretty radical notion. Upcycled and recycled fashion is merely one expression of that notion, but one with such a wealth of talent and creativity that it warrants a book of its own.

I am part of a movement to inform and share information about activism in fashion. It started because I felt that eco-fashion had reached a tipping point where the best of the best could be judged against the mainstream industry, yet still carried the stigma of hemp clothing sold at a head shop. It became equally important for me to reveal the hidden price tag of fast fashion, as a means to promote conscious consumerism. In a way it is an outgrowth of the 99% and Occupy movements,[2] an attempt to shake up the industry with grass-roots activist information, and with intellectual and cutting-edge design. As a designer by trade, it is just as important that I inspire as well as challenge.

Why fashion? The clothing, textiles and associated support industries employ one-sixth of the world's population, from growing cotton crops to finishing garments. So if you thought fashion was not saving babies, think again: it has the power to change the world!

1 Published online at: www.defra.gov.uk
2 The 99% and Occupy movements are grass-roots activist groups that protest the imbalance of wealth and power. The name 99% refers to the 1 per cent of top earners and the financial burden they are felt to have inflicted on the other 99 per cent of the population. The Occupy movement, which is against social and economic inequality, started in protest against investment bankers and CEOs and the part they played in the recession.

Raggedy

DESIGNERS WORKING WITH USED MATERIALS

Silent People

With its origins in the 'make-do-and-mend' mentality of our grandparents, recycled and vintage clothing has long been in vogue with the fashion fringe and avant-garde. The history of upcycled vintage clothing is firmly based on the reimagining and redesigning of good-quality but worn or stained items of clothing.

There has of late, however, been an explosion of designers working with less conventional materials – table linen, flour sacks, mattress ticking and military tents – piecing and patching them into individual high-fashion and accessories collections. The nature of the materials and the processes involved make each piece unique, individually conceived and crafted from scratch, with different fabrics and configurations used each time. In a fast-fashion world of throwaway clothing, recycled design is the ultimate expression of slow fashion.

The beauty and attraction of recycled clothing and accessories lies in their ready-made past – the history and heritage that accompany those textiles and imbue them with a sense of value. In a consumer-driven society of fast fashion, where we have lost our material connection to clothing, the use and reuse of vintage textiles and garments brings with it a tactile story, a knowledge of where it came from – in some cases, who wore it, in others an imagined history. We surround ourselves with textiles twenty-four hours a day, from the moment we rise and dress until the moment we drop off to sleep comforted by our duvet.

We work hard to pay for those textiles that are interwoven into the most intimate moments of our life, yet we know nothing about them. How was it spun, woven or knitted, and by whom? How many carbon-dioxide emissions did it clock up making its way to our wardrobe? We only focus on how it looks once it is complete. Were we to ask how it was made, we would discover that an average of 2000 chemicals[1] are used in the production of a modern textile, from the chemicals it takes to grow the fibre to the chemicals used to dye the finished textile, several of which are known carcinogens and listed by the United States Environmental Protection Agency (EPA) as category one or two dangerous chemicals. Reusing vintage textiles from a simpler time is one way of eliminating some of these from our lives.

Of the 30.8kg (68lbs) of clothing and textiles that the average American throws away each year, about 85 per cent of it is destined for landfill.[2] In the UK alone, over one million tonnes of clothing is thrown away each year.[3] Textiles present a particular problem in landfill: synthetics do not decompose within a scalable timeline; and wool emits methane during decomposition, which is a key contributor to greenhouse gases. In addition, the export of used and discarded clothing to the African continent has devastated its fledgling textile and apparel industries. Furthermore, the garbage crises, from which many cities suffer, make the diversion of materials from landfill absolutely vital. This has not been lost on fashion's mainstream, with many celebrities choosing to wear vintage over new on the red carpet. For its annual Curiosity Pop-Up Shop, famous UK charity shop Oxfam embeds Quick Response (QR) codes[4] in items donated by celebrities, offering snippets of the garment's history. The authenticity and heritage imbued in second-hand items goes well beyond monetary value alone.

The area of recycle, reuse and redesign is a particularly vibrant and rich source for innovative creation, with a range of designers working with recycled fabrics, garments, hardware and more, diverting post-consumer waste from landfill and reinvigorating these used materials with new life and value.

1 Hazardous Substance Research Centers – Environmental Update #24, published online at: www.hsrcssw.org/update24.pdf
2 Earth911, published online at: earth911.com/recycling/household/clothing-and-textile/facts-about-clothes
3 Published online at: www.defra.gov.uk
4 Quick Response codes are two-dimensional barcodes that can be read by smartphones.

MAYER Peace Collection

2ETN

NECKLACES FASHIONED FROM
STERLING SILVER AND VINTAGE
CZECH GLASS ARE DECORATED WITH
HAND-PAINTED ACRYLIC BIRDS.

In the spirit of American portraiture and mourning miniatures of the 1700s to 1800s, 2ETN crafts one-of-a-kind artworks with graphite, oils and acrylics, framed by found antiques, reclaimed precious metals and ethically sourced or vintage stones. The belief that precious stones and metals are not the sole elements from which jewelry derives its value informs the designers' philosophy; they show reverence to the past and the present, while using nature and history as their guide. Their pieces embody a dark melancholy romanticism, reminiscent of *Bram Stoker's Dracula*, and worthy of any period drama's leading lady. With titles such as 'Sleep of Death', 'Deathmask Moth' and 'A Young Albrecht', mostly monochromatic miniatures portray a vintage hourglass, a chalice, skull, snake or any number of birds, bees and bugs, each one beautifully depicted. These hang from amber, topaz and metal beads or are framed by tiny intricate oxidized metal and silver borders or rough-cut crystal and Czech glass – all artfully formed into chokers, cuffs and rings.

2ETN's inspiration also comes from an appreciation for slow processes and pure craftsmanship. The label's name derives from the fusion of the phonetic pronunciation of Pamela's last name (2E) and Edward's initials (ETN). Their proudest achievement is that they have been able to stay

AN ORIGINAL 1930S EISENBERG
BROOCH IS REFASHIONED INTO
A NECKLACE EMBELLISHED WITH
A HAND-PAINTED ACRYLIC SKULL.

rue to their values; they have never mass-produced anything and source all their materials responsibly. The entire jewelry line is produced in the USA, right down to the boxes.

Both from working-class backgrounds, Tuohy and Novinsky set up shop in Land Park, Sacramento, where they grow their own food, ride their bikes, shop locally and have easy access to the natural beauty of northern California. Fighting the tide of commercialism through its work, 2ETN believes that the stories woven into its pieces are of greater value than any precious stone; that the time and effort involved in hand-painting a miniature or carefully sourcing and pairing vintage beads far outweighs the quick and easy option of using a single giant stone. The designers interlace life and love, joy and sadness, friendship, respect and power in their creative process.

Admiring Native American philosophy, 2ETN donates a percentage of all jewelry sales to the Pine Ridge Reservation's Adopt-A-Buffalo Campaign. By supporting the traditional ecology, economy and culture surrounding the buffalo, it hopes to honour the part Native Americans played as the first indigenous people to live on the North American continent. Through the revival of traditional ways of life and the rebuilding of buffalo herds, the label is helping to rebalance the ugly history between native and settler, giving back to the land that sustains them.

Producing remarkable and original jewelry, Tuohy and Novinsky often show their work in a gallery setting. Since opening its own studio in 2010, 2ETN has built a worldwide following of collectors. Pieces can be bought from Grange Hall in Dallas and online at Project Artisan; custom-made pieces can be ordered directly from the website.

CRESTED EAGLE CHOKER IN STERLING
SILVER, CZECH GLASS, ROUGH-CUT
CRYSTAL AND HAND-PAINTED ACRYLICS.

ARTEMAS QUIBBLE AND THE CREATURES OF MME DU BARRY

JASON ROSS PRODUCES AN AUTHENTIC ARTISANAL ACCESSORIES COLLECTION, UNLIKE ANYTHING YOU WILL SEE ANYWHERE ELSE.

INDIVIDUALLY FINISHED AND AGED LEATHER SATCHELS AND SADDLE BAGS HAVE AN OLD-SCHOOL APPEAL.

A mix of antiquity and rough-hewn sophistication, his pieces resonate with the soul. He works with reclaimed materials laden with historical and utilitarian use. They are given a new lease of life through his handcraft label Artemas Quibble and the Creatures of Mme du Barry. Reminiscent of an old-world blacksmith or saddle maker, Ross channels generations of artistry through his material choice and his own talent. His body of work includes a range of bags that look like something Robin Hood would have gifted Maid Marian, made with love from traditional materials by a gifted artisan.

Working with items such as sixteenth-century leather book covers and vintage finials, Ross remakes them into a belt, necklace or cuff. His materials look like they have experienced many hard and well-loved lives, bravely and proudly bearing the scars from those lives, before making their way to Ross's skilled hands and enriching each of his pieces with their past. 'So much work has already been put into my pieces by people who weren't necessarily appreciated or respected. I'm able to showcase their work and give it a new life.' Ross's work always begins with a reclaimed piece, employing its unique artisanal nature to inform the new design. Some items remain unique, while others are produced to scale through the 3000-year-old process of lost-wax casting, which respects the scratches and scars each piece bears, while using recycled metals. Ancient leather is mimicked through a work-intensive 20-step process of aging raw American cowhide with vegetable tanning agents.

Saddlebags have thonged edgings, hefty brass buckles and rivets from vintage finds, with a patina that took a lifetime to achieve. The heavy, well-worn leather brings a richness to Ross's work that cannot be achieved by dye alone. The gently warped and worn leather marries beautifully with the iron and brass workmen's tools reimagined as bag handles and clasps – a new life, bringing a new meaning and a new value to underappreciated materials. With a love and respect for history and tradition, Ross brings a modern sensibility to ancient finds in his Brooklyn studio. Scouting for objects that inspire him, Ross lives with their past until they speak to him of their future. They hang on his studio walls until it is their turn to be reinvented (often prompted by a looming deadline): 'Every found object tells a story, what it was used for, why it was there. It's very exciting to piece it all together.'

Donna Karan is one of Ross's admirers, and she stocks his work in her Urban Zen store in New York's Manhattan, as well as showcasing it on the catwalk. She is rarely seen without one of his 1.83m (6 feet) long strips of embellished leather wound around her wrist, and describes his work as 'raw, sexy and artistic' as well as 'personal objects of desire you'll own forever'. Every piece of handcrafted leather that Ross fashions features embellishments in silver and brass, each one skillfully made from scratch with his handmade tools. Each item is distinctive and unique, resonating with the soulful history of the reclaimed elements from which they are made. Ross considers his work 'a celebration of what has been lost', and a means by which he can honour the nameless artisans who first created the materials he now reinvents.

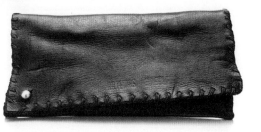

ATELIER AWASH

ITALIANS DAVIDE GRAZIOLI AND MAURO PAVESI FOUNDED ATELIER AWASH, A SUSTAINABLE MENSWEAR FASHION LABEL, IN BERLIN IN 2007.

The collection is based on classic and timeless design, inspired by contemporary cultural explorers, the characteristics of which the partners share. Each item within the collection reflects a relaxed and stylish approach to fashion, mirroring the aesthetic background of artist and designer Davide Grazioli, and influenced by his trips around the globe, from Japan to Africa. An internationally renowned artist, Grazioli works in diverse media, with sustainability and the environment a consistent focus for his artworks as well as his collection. The relaxed look is reminiscent of the crumpled elegance of Humphrey Bogart in the film *Casablanca*, with natural pale linen suits and unbuttoned and untucked shirts.

Colours range from off-white to rich dark organic tones, including henna, dirt and, of course, the ubiquitous black – the pieces are designed by an Italian after all. As a collection of classics, the styling remains consistent. Grazioli is not interested in trends and fads; the colours, textures and fabrics create the variation. Each piece is realized in a range of fabrics, including 100 per cent recycled carded wool, reclaimed, end-of-life fabric finds and Italian organic materials such as cotton, linen and hemp, all vegetable-dyed and Global Organic Textile Standard (GOTS) certified.

Atelier Awash's story began with long journeys in Africa to find organic and fair-trade partners. It ends back in Italy, where the label now undertakes all its production, supporting the ailing Italian family-owned manufacturing heritage. Atelier Awash is hypersensitive to environmental problems and from the outset has practised its craft with care and responsibility. The collection incorporates Cardato Rigenerato, a regenerated carbon-dioxide-neutral

THE 'ONE NIGHT IN TOKYO' SUIT BLAZER, MADE FROM THICK RECYCLED CARDED WOOL, WAS INSPIRED BY A JOURNEY THROUGH JAPAN.

THE CLASSIC, CERTIFIED-ORGANIC BLAZER
'ONE NIGHT IN ADDIS' AND THE 'BOYS
DON'T CRY' CASUAL TROUSERS EPITOMIZE
THE ATELIER AWASH AESTHETIC OF EASY
WASH, WEAR AND TRAVEL.

carded wool fibre, certified by the Prato Chamber of Commerce. The wool, obtained from used fabrics and clothes, is the first zero-impact textile product. This is achieved by calculating carbon emissions and purchasing credits to offset these emissions, so that the factory can function as carbon neutral. Interestingly, there is a hundred-year practice of regenerating wool – cashmere, angora, alpaca and mohair – in the Prato district. The process is labour intensive, requiring the collection of fabric offcuts and used clothing, sorting them by quality and colour, cleaning and removing all attachments such as zips and buttons, before they can be shredded, respun and, finally, rewoven.

The label also produces a collection of handwoven and vegetable-dyed silk and cotton scarves made in partnership with a small Ethiopian farm whose goal is to support underprivileged women and to protect regional heritage on an artisanal level. Furthermore, Atelier Awash upcycles its own waste into a range of casual travellers' hats. The company is a member of MADE BY, a Dutch organization that links some of the most relevant sustainable fashion labels, and is a firm believer in the cradle-to-cradle philosophy of William McDonough and Michael Braungart. Highly critical of upcycling second-hand poor-quality garments, Grazioli carefully considers each purchase, weighing the ethical and ecological advantages and disadvantages prior to finalizing material decisions.

CEEBEE

CARMEN BJÖRNALD CREATES
A LINE OF ACCESSORIES
USING RECYCLED MATERIALS
FROM NATURAL AND
ORGANIC ORIGINS.

A collector of everything, Björnald has an insatiable appetite for beauty, especially that found in unused and discarded objects. Friends, family and neighbours regularly donate items to this magpie collector, who often receives emails from complete strangers with offers to investigate their loft, garage or storage space. With careful respect for the environment, the low-impact CeeBee collection is produced locally in support of low-income families through labour creation, almost entirely from discarded and undervalued materials.

German-born Björnald grew up in Sweden, graduating with a degree in fabric research and design. With a background as a musician as well as a high-fashion model, Björnald now lives and works in Italy. After taking a jewelry course conducted by contemporary sculptor Davide de Paoli, renowned for his work with precious metals mixed with minor materials, Björnald created her first jewelry collection with a loom, a knitting needle and a crochet hook. The pieces were created by weaving silver threads with precious and semi-precious stones through a range of irregular and unique shapes.

Often inspired by the material itself, Björnald spent some time trying to find out what happened to retired hot-air balloons after a long-awaited flight in one. Her research finally paid off when two balloons were delivered – a whole new source of material. The pieces made from this material carry a tag with the name of the balloon, the number of flight hours it logged and the donor.

THE DIANA TOTE IS MADE
FROM RECYCLED PAPER SEALED
WITH RESIN, WITH BAMBOO
HANDLES AND ITS OWN JUTE
STORAGE BAG.

NECKLACE AND MATCHING BRACELET
MADE FROM TIGHTLY ROLLED PAPER
STRIPS THREADED TOGETHER WITH
SILVER WIRE AND BEADS.

BAGS AND LAPTOP BRIEFCASES
ARE CREATED FROM LAMINATED
AND PLEATED RECYCLED
PAPER STRIPS.

OPPOSITE: RECYCLED PRINTED
PAGES ARE APPLIED TO WOOD
BY DECOUPAGE AND THEN
PROTECTED WITH RESIN TO
MAKE THE BELL PENDANT.

DESIGNERS WORKING WITH USED MATERIALS

Travel made Björnald aware of the global problem of waste and led to the development of her line of accessories produced solely from waste materials. Her one-of-a-kind 'Paper Collection' of handbags, backpacks, shoppers, pouches, belts and jewelry is all made from the pages of old fashion magazines, maps, newspapers, comics and even old yellowed notebooks found in a friend's loft. The paper comes from different parts of the world, is meticulously selected based on colour and image use, cut into strips, laminated and woven, pleated and carefully finished. Items have internal pockets, precious handles or are layered between non-toxic plastic to transform them into bags for every occasion.

The 'Plastic 4ever' accessories are made entirely out of plastic shopping bags, collected by women and sold by weight, through Onlus, a company that specializes in the development of a technique to modify plastic materials through heat pressing. FSC wooden spheres are covered with recycled paper using decoupage, a process that layers cut images on to another surface, to create the jewelry. Designs are mixed with nickel-free 925 sterling silver to create a line of timeless jewelry. CeeBee's followers are rewarded every time with unexpected finds.

CHRISTOPHER RAEBURN

USING RE-APPROPRIATED
MILITARY FABRICS, BRITISH
FASHION DESIGNER
CHRISTOPHER RAEBURN
IS KNOWN FOR CREATING
ORIGINAL, ETHICALLY AWARE
MENS- AND WOMENSWEAR
COLLECTIONS, WITH A FOCUS
ON OUTERWEAR.

Raeburn specializes in garments that are functional, intelligent and meticulously crafted, as well as proudly 'Remade in England'. His extreme attention to detail is reminiscent of the care and considered functionality found in military uniforms, the overstock and overruns of which are his base material. The pieces are crafted and reworked from an array of materials, including Swedish camouflage tank Tyvek, forty-year-old army snowsuits, Royal Air Force-issue windproof cotton flying suits, Virgin Airways hot-air balloons, firemen's protective clothing and Eurostar train uniforms. Raeburn's workwear aesthetic is counterbalanced by his incongruous use of colour, proportion and layering. He reinterprets modern, youthful, urban, ecological design from a utilitarian perspective, resulting in clothes that are iconically English in their sense of good British design.

The collection is broken down into three main capsules. Raeburn fashions wool bomber jackets and coats from scraps of patchworked battledress in a contemporary take on urban militia. A line of hoodies and parkas is made entirely from British-milled, end-of-line cotton stock, both pure and rubberized. Luminous and mesmerizingly translucent hooded jackets and parkas make up the third range. They feature fine taped seams that overlap and intersect to form intricate patterns, creating a graphic effect on the sheer parachute silk and the Virgin Airways hot-air balloons. Most designs roll up and fit into tiny coordinating bags and pouches.

Raeburn spends a significant amount of time searching and researching fabrics for his 'Remade in England' collection, a pivotal focus for his line. Careful to source materials available in large enough quantities to produce his orders, he now works with ends and dead stock from the British cotton mills. The Victorinox collaboration saw Raeburn and the makers of the Original Swiss Army Knife create the 'Remade in Switzerland' capsule collection for Autumn/Winter 11/12. The thoughtful, technical and, as always,

THE WPCP PARACHUTE CROPPED
PARKA IS MADE FROM REPURPOSED
PARACHUTES AND ROLLS UP INTO
A TINY TOGGLE CLOSURE POUCH.

utilitarian designs were accompanied by an amazing stop-motion video by Swiss graphic designer Silvio Ketterer, with raw materials organizing themselves while Raeburn deconstructs and reconstructs items on the sewing machine. Lightweight, nylon jackets are complemented by heavy, hooded waterproof jackets and an iconic Swiss Red Cross hood scarf. Swiss Army Knives handily placed in pockets and on zip pulls all carry the Swiss Red Cross.

A graduate from London's prestigious Royal College of Art in 2006, Raeburn became known for his pioneering work in non-traditional upcycled materials. He was also asked to participate in an exhibition at the Imperial

War Museum in London entitled 'Camouflage' in 2007. Launched in 2008, his label has received multiple accolades and has won London Fashion Week's NEWGEN Designer of the Year Award several times. Raeburn collaborated with British designer Tim Soar on a 2009 menswear collection showcased at Paris Men's Fashion Week, and works on capsule collections with upcycling company Worn Again that sell around the world.

PIECES FROM THE SCORCH
FREEZE COLLECTION, SO CALLED
BECAUSE OF THE FIRE-RETARDANT
AND COLD-WEATHER-PROTECTIVE
FABRICS USED.

CLARE BARE

A BROOKLYN-BASED ARTIST
AND DESIGNER, CLARE BARE
SPECIALIZES IN ECO-FRIENDLY
LINGERIE AND SWIMWEAR
MADE FROM VINTAGE FABRICS,
ORGANIC COTTON
AND BAMBOO JERSEY.

All Clare's pieces are made by hand in limited-edition runs, and are structured to naturally flatter the body without the use of constrictive and restrictive hardware. Her retro-inspired designs embody a sensuality from days gone by, featuring high waists, broad contrasting elastic straps and sexually alluring criss-cross bands and suspenders. Cut-out shapes, sheer inserts and gently contrasting matt, sheer and shiny fabrics all contribute to the appeal. Eschewing the use of underwiring and boning, her designs have soft cups and softly gathered bikini bottoms. Her collection plays the dual roles of retro sensual seductress and flirty playful minx, reflecting Clare's diverse tastes, which range from tacky neon charity-shop toys to fine wine and oysters.

An avid fan of vintage textiles of all types, Clare started her collection of textiles while at college and experimenting with printmaking. At one stage, it was piled so high that she was left with no space to work. So, Clare Herron conceived Clare Bare to give her piles of fabric a purpose and to make clever use of her nickname (originally Clare Bear). She explains: 'When searching for vintage fabrics, I gravitate toward anything that jumps out at me, and I usually go without a plan and end up with a concept for a collection by the time I leave. I also look for solids that are soft and drape well.'

Growing up next to a charity-shop warehouse, Clare constantly stocked up on mismatched china, old picture frames and fabric ends for her creative experiments in mosaics, collage and bikini making. With a particular penchant for prints from the 1960s and 1970s, and anything floral or psychedelic, Clare has fabric from a diverse range of uses, including vintage linen, curtains, nighties and pillowcases. Most are sourced from charity shops on road trips, but, occasionally, she has been the recipient of defunct factory stock and end-of-line materials from manufacturers in upstate New York, who have donated lingerie silk and mesh. Clare dyes and silk-screen prints the single-colour fabrics with her original prints, using her natural dye treatments that incorporate lac and logwood.

MATCHING SCRUNCH BRALETTE AND
BLOOMERS MADE FROM 4-PLY HEAVY SILK
WITH BLACK PICOT EDGE ELASTIC.

Textiles are at the centre of Clare's work, and she designs her whole collection around her fabric finds. Even her own prints and colour schemes are based on her vintage discoveries. Her valued vintage finds make her limited-edition pieces the bedrock of her collection, with many of her garments made to order and taking two to four weeks to produce. Working with clients one on one, Clare loves to make others comfortable about themselves and their bodies. She revels in their personal stories, acting somewhere between a therapist, a personal advisor and a made-to-measure designer, putting the intimate back into intimate apparel.

THE COLLECTION IS DESIGNED AROUND HIGH-IMPACT PRINTS AND SATURATED NATURAL DYES ON BAMBOO JERSEY AND VINTAGE MESH.

A STRETCH MESH ROMPER WITH
BLACK LACE PANELS IS WORN
WITH A KIMONO ROBE IN HEAVY,
HAND-DYED 4-PLY SILK.

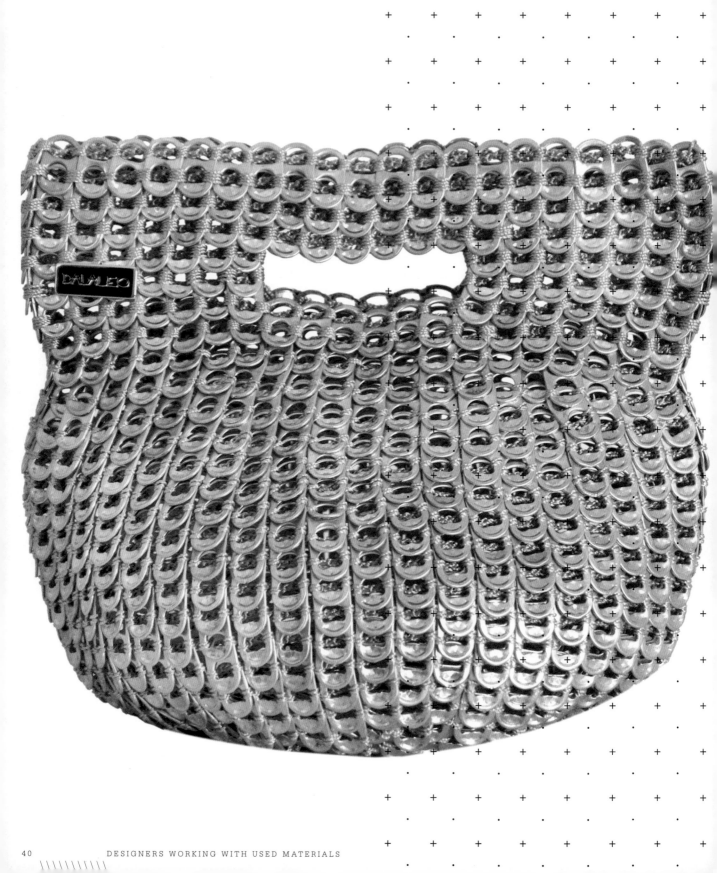

DALALEO

FOUNDED IN 1998 BY
LUISA LEONARDI SCOMAZZONI,
OTHERWISE KNOWN
AS LEO, DALALEO IS BASED
AROUND A PASSION FOR
RESEARCH AND IS A
CELEBRATION OF CREATIVITY
AND HANDCRAFT.

Dalaleo is renowned for its collection of bags and accessories handmade in Italy and Brazil from a combination of aluminum can ring pulls and fine crochet work. The collection is the outgrowth of a Brazilian holiday, and the purchase of a bag produced locally in the favelas of Salvador de Bahia. Brazilian creativity has long been based on a culture of inventive make do and mend, with a range of locally made items for sale at any market, and made from otherwise unwanted and worthless materials. For example, there are doormats made from bottle tops, cushion covers made from a series of knotted salvaged fabric scraps and bags made from a combination of crochet and aluminum can ring pulls. This single product, combined with intensive and passionate research and development, forms the basis of the Dalaleo collection.

At first unaware of the true value of her purchase, Leo later realized that the men she saw rummaging through rubbish were collecting aluminum cans for recycling, thereby generating some income for their families in the favela. The ring pulls from these cans were then removed so that other family members could create products for sale at local markets. Dalaleo bags stand out from local artisanal production owing to their

DALALEO BAGS AND PURSES ARE
HAND-CROCHETED IN BRAZIL AND
ENTIRELY PRODUCED FROM SALVAGED
SOFT-DRINK CAN RING PULLS.

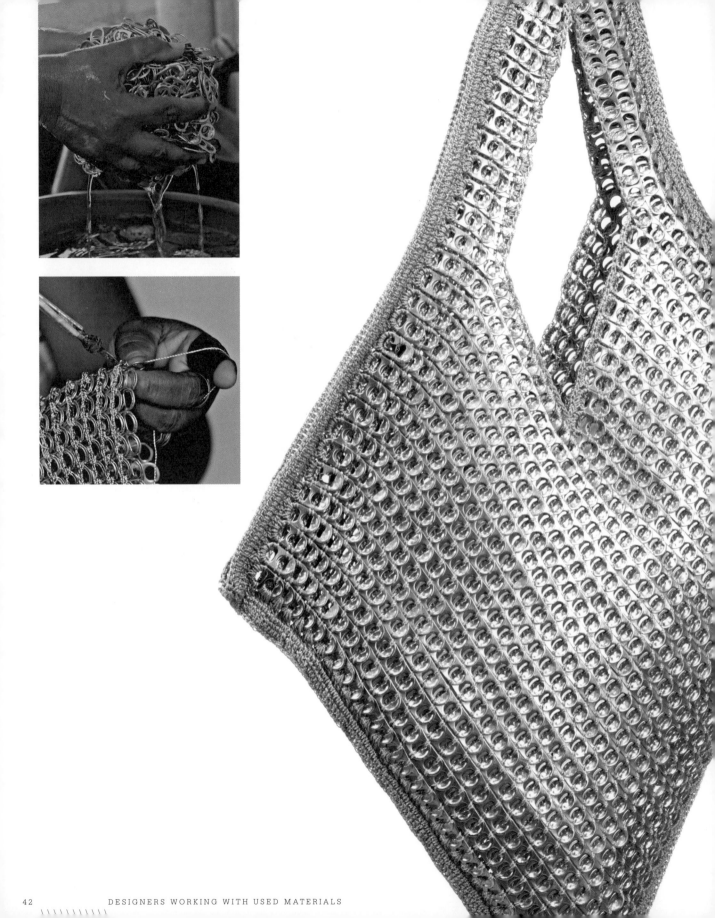

DESIGNERS WORKING WITH USED MATERIALS

unique design, a high level of taste and strict quality control of both materials and technique. The production process begins with the collection or purchase of aluminum ring pulls and is followed by careful selection, hammering, washing, polishing and drying – all before any crochet happens.

Brazil is a country of artisans and craftspeople, some traditional, others imported, where women have long made the most of their creative skill sets to use waste, decorate their homes and generate income. The burgeoning favelas play host to this rich culture, housing everything from the famous samba drummers to Capoeira schools and sewing cooperatives, alongside gangs, violence and drugs. Using this fertile base of local craftspeople, Dalaleo carefully constructs, sews and crochets the range of bags, purses and jewelry, employing premium-quality crochet yarn and other materials such as leather and jersey. The stories of the men and women who collect and produce the Dalaleo bags are woven into every piece, enriching the value of each item beyond their obvious visual significance.

The Dalaleo showroom is the outgrowth of Leo's passion and personal expression, where fashion accessories are mixed with high-level ethnic style. Leo travels extensively for research purposes, the most recent result of which was the launch of 'Dalaleo by Michela Bruni', a capsule collection of necklaces and bracelets entirely handmade in Italy. Aluminum can ring pulls from Dalaleo's Brazilian production and end-of-line and offcut jersey and other recovered fabrics are fashioned into a highly desirable jewelry collection, which perfectly complements the label's bags. Dalaleo was the only accessories brand to be selected to show at the Paris Who's Next Prêt-à-Porter fashion show in 2012.

DALALEO BY MICHELA BRUNI IS A CAPSULE COLLECTION OF HANDMADE NECKLACES AND BRACELETS CREATED FROM ALUMINUM RING PULLS IN COMBINATION WITH UPCYCLED TEXTILE WASTE.

DESIGNERS WORKING WITH USED MATERIALS

DENHAM

With a profound respect for history and craft, Denham the Jeanmaker has built a men's and women's luxury denim collection without rival. Jason Denham is the single-minded founder of the company, whose obsession with denim continues to inspire the brand today. He holds the conviction that deep knowledge only comes with extensive research, and that legacy remains central to the brand's identity and design approach. Denham knows its predecessors, its contemporaries and its competition. It operates with no bounds to its inspiration, and has never been content to merely reproduce what is already available, like so many in the denim industry. Using research to feed its passion to progress tradition, the label benefits richly from the tailoring traditions it studies and worships.

One of the many unique features of the brand is its garment library, which supplies the company with the raw materials for its research and its design and development. Decades in the making, the Denham Garment Library is a rich and diverse source of denim jeans, military apparel, travel gear and utilitarian workwear, dating back to the last century. This is not acquisition for the sake of it, but acquisition to examine, to analyze and to learn from our past and our heritage of garment and textile production. Each item in the library represents a starting point for a collection. As Denham says: 'Before we created we collected.'

WOMEN'S JACKETS ARE PRODUCED IN HIGHLY LIMITED EDITIONS FROM VINTAGE JAPANESE AND INDOCHINESE TEXTILES.

THE CAMINO RE-CUT JACKET DEMONSTRATES A LABORIOUS ATTENTION TO DETAIL, WITH BONED AND BOUND SEAMS AND HOOK AND EYE CLOSURES.

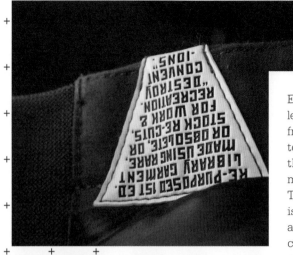

Each season, Denham endeavours to create at least one flagship style that uses fabrics re-cut from historically, culturally or ethnically significant textiles. The company recycles the rich narratives that live within the warp and weave of these materials as well as the materials themselves. The diverse results of this historic research is incorporated into Denham's own design ethic, and reinterpreted into a blend of tradition and contemporary design and use. This balance of the ancient, ethnic and modern makes for a stunning mix, rooted in equal respect for all three. Such fruitful collaborative design explorations have produced core items in a range of vintage and contemporary textile combinations. Successful completion requires a true partnership between the designers, development team, manufacturers and suppliers: a true labour of love.

The process starts by identifying the source of inspiration for the forthcoming collection and results in a team trek to the location, where they undertake comprehensive sweeps of local workwear, military clothing and weekend markets. Following meetings with specialized traders of contemporary and antique textiles, the team acquires enough fabric and/or garments to reconstruct a highly limited range. Limited-edition jackets have been produced in Indochinese hill-tribe narrow-loom textiles; 100-year-old patched Japanese 'Boro' textiles; Dutch army ponchos and blankets; antique French bed linen and World War II silk parachutes – each one to unique and amazing effect. Each season's creative adventures further Denham's tradition and honour its past.

JEFFREY WANG

WORKING WITH BRANDING, GRAPHIC DESIGN, VISUAL STYLING, FASHION, PHOTOGRAPHY, FILM, ADVERTISING, WEBSITE DESIGN AND CURATION, JEFFREY WANG HAS PRODUCED MANY PROJECTS THAT SHOWCASE HIS BROAD-BASED TALENTS AS A CREATIVE DIRECTOR.

THE PURPOSE OF THE PERSONA COLLECTION WAS TO CREATE WEARABLE ART FROM RECYCLED JEANS, USING ONLY SAFETY PINS TO HOLD THE PIECES TOGETHER.

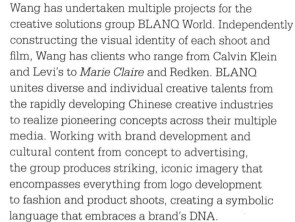

Combining the worlds of art, fashion and film, Wang has undertaken multiple projects for the creative solutions group BLANQ World. Independently constructing the visual identity of each shoot and film, Wang has clients who range from Calvin Klein and Levi's to *Marie Claire* and Redken. BLANQ unites diverse and individual creative talents from the rapidly developing Chinese creative industries to realize pioneering concepts across their multiple media. Working with brand development and cultural content from concept to advertising, the group produces striking, iconic imagery that encompasses everything from logo development to fashion and product shoots, creating a symbolic language that embraces a brand's DNA.

Wang's innovative work includes a collaborative project with iconic denim jeans producer Levi Strauss and the Taiwanese Fubon Art Foundation. With a brief to redesign recycled customer-donated Levi Strauss jeans into wearable art sculptures, Wang carefully constructed the denim into expressive and poetic pieces with only the aid of safety pins, to incredible result. The work, entitled 'Persona', highlighted the raw character and personality of the denim, showcasing the material in all its beauty and variation. It incorporated jeans in every shade and at every stage of wear, tear and fade, ranging from darkest indigo blue to acid-wash white, and from pristine to tattered and patched. As no jeans were deconstructed, cut or sewn, it will be possible to dismantle the sculptures and wear each pair of jeans again, without damage or evidence of their flight of fancy. The temporary nature of the project allowed for a truly recycled and recyclable project.

DESIGNERS WORKING WITH USED MATERIALS

The carefully constructed wearable sculptures express a poetry and elegance not usually associated with utilitarian workaday jeans. Variations in style, cut and size create an overall unity through their very multiplicity and diversity. Highly sophisticated conceptual shapes cocoon, adorn and play with the female form, alternately obscuring and revealing, exaggerating and extending. The project is beautifully illustrated on BLANQ World's website, with a stop-motion film showing the creative project in its entirety from the construction of the photoshoot to the final expressive images.

THE USED DENIM JEANS SOURCED FOR THE PROJECT RUN ACROSS A BROAD RANGE OF WEAR AND TEAR, IN AN EFFORT TO TRULY CAPTURE THE BREADTH AND DIVERSITY OF DENIM CULTURE.

JULIA BARBEE

*'I CREATE BECAUSE
I AM CREATED.'*

The body of Julia Barbee's work is a visual, literary and olfactory journey of investigation, observation, creation and art. Drawing inspiration from folk tales and history, Barbee deconstructs tactile ephemera, woollen fibre and gossamer to create extraordinary clothing designs. She explores the story of the garment industry through vintage couture hems and tatting, delicately and poetically piecing her finds together in an entirely new creation. She composes new forms from old, dancing her materials back to life, while endeavouring to be a steward of the environment in some small way. Barbee's designs favour a neutral palette, with the elimination of colour and contrast, forcing texture and detail to dominate her output. Her alternatively ghostly and whimsical pieces are made with a magpie's eye for shiny, glittering finds, often bound in a nest of thread, ribbon and beads. Her theatrical styling is somewhere between dream and nightmare, fantasy and reality.

Formally trained as a sculptor, Barbee uses her instruction to shape her clothing creations on the human body, working with a sculptor's sensibility in three dimensions. Her pieces possess a poetry and romanticism that is ethereal. Sourcing her materials from myriad locales, including flea markets and garage sales, she also receives donations, and relishes simply finding materials in unexpected places. Working from

existing garments, Barbee discards all that does not catch her eye, while salvaging all that does. Her sourcing and raw materials act as her inspiration, with stores of material to help her to connect the dots between form and line, balance and body. Although a talented artist, Barbee never sketches her designs; instead, she plunders her treasure trove of goodies, allowing designs to float around in her head for weeks before realizing them.

Barbee never planned to be a designer – she merely started making clothes, and it went on from there. Originally inspired by deconstructed Stella McCartney pieces, she decided to try her hand at something similar, ending up with a capsule collection of around 15 pieces, which she consigned to a local boutique in Portland, Oregon. Barbee's practice incorporates far more than recycled clothing and upcycled designs; it catalogues her life as performance, and she records

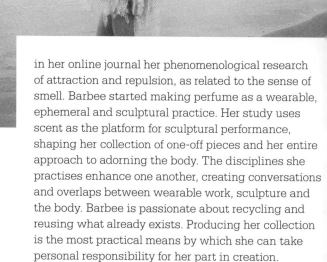

in her online journal her phenomenological research of attraction and repulsion, as related to the sense of smell. Barbee started making perfume as a wearable, ephemeral and sculptural practice. Her study uses scent as the platform for sculptural performance, shaping her collection of one-off pieces and her entire approach to adorning the body. The disciplines she practises enhance one another, creating conversations and overlaps between wearable work, sculpture and the body. Barbee is passionate about recycling and reusing what already exists. Producing her collection is the most practical means by which she can take personal responsibility for her part in creation.

ECLECTIC FOUND MATERIALS FORM
THE INSPIRATION AND SOURCE FOR
ALL OF JULIA BARBEE'S WORK.

THE COCOONING BLANKET COAT
(LEFT) HAS A MEN'S SUITING LAPEL
CLOSURE AND KNIT RIB CUFFS.

THE SLEEVELESS VEST (RIGHT)
IS MADE FROM MULTIPLE JACKET
LAPELS LAYERED ONE ON TOP
OF ANOTHER.

JUNKY STYLING

TIMELESS, DECONSTRUCTED, RE-CUT AND COMPLETELY TRANSFORMED SUSTAINABLE FASHION AND ACCESSORIES FOR WOMEN AND MEN ARE CREATED BY JUNKY STYLING.

Self-taught designers Annika Sanders and Kerry Seager founded the innovative label in 1997. With no background in fashion, they were inspired by their travels and observations of recycling around the world. The charity-shop culture in San Francisco and the neat boxes of recycled glass, plastic and paper in the basement of their apartment building sparked their business concept of upcycling clothing.

With a focus on individuality, no two garments are the same. Born of resourcefulness, the company specializes in producing its designs from the highest quality second-hand clothing, as well as from pre-consumer damaged goods, decommissioned military gear, T-shirts, knitwear, trench coats and denim. Reworking men's suits and shirts into experimental yet playful womenswear, the duo manage to walk a fine line between cutting-edge design and playful flirtatiousness. Junky Styling has been described as producing 'an eccentrically chic line of mutant couture' by *The New Yorker*, and as 'high fashion street couture' by British *Vogue*.

The exposed studio and store space in The Old Truman Brewery off Brick Lane in London reflects Junky Styling's pioneering and transparent work practices. Taking recycled, worn, discarded and second-hand clothing, Junky identifies the existing form and details of its raw material, and then reinterprets it into an entirely new design. With a preference for working with natural fibres and, in particular, men's old sturdy wool suits, Junky Styling extends the life of items by changing and updating their construction. With their studio located close to the heart of the city, the designers make an intriguing and alternative commentary on the 'nine-to-five' materials they use for their avant-garde designs.

Over more than ten years, Junky Styling has developed a solid reputation for fusing original, timeless British design with ethics. The partners aim to make every fashion consumer view clothing in a different way, recognizing the recyclable potential from the perspective of investing in quality fabric and durability of design. Leading this area of eco-design and breaking new ground with its edgy, contemporary upcycling, Junky also offers a bespoke service under the name Wardrobe Surgery, where customers can bring in items from their own wardrobe to be transformed into an entirely new look.

Spreading the recycled love, Junky shares its knowledge and experience. The designers have published a combined history and how-to book entitled *Junky Styling – Wardrobe Surgery*, and are founding members of the Ethical Fashion Forum. They participate in museum presentations around the world, and fashion education programmes are a growing means of communicating their ethos to the next generation of designers and consumers. Recipients of the RSPCA Good Business Award for Fashion, owing to their emphasis on sustainability and use of ethically sourced materials, they were also awarded support from the British Fashion Council and were named Eco Heroes by *The Guardian* newspaper.

KM/A

VIENNESE LABEL KM/A FUSES FASHION, ART AND PERFORMANCE, WHILE PRODUCING A BEAUTIFUL, FUNCTIONAL AND WEARABLE COLLECTION.

Founders Katha Harrer and Michael Ellinger produce a collection as timeless as it is beautiful. Non-traditional, discarded and end-of-life materials are used to handcraft unique pieces that carry the signature of Harrer's personal style. Employing a range of materials, including roofing paper, rice and postal shipping bags, prison blankets, windsurf sails and decommissioned parachutes, Harrer often sources materials directly from prisons and army outlets, as well as at flea markets and second-hand stores. The designers make an antithetical statement to the fashion system's sense of conformity and means of mass production. The company logo of a clock symbolizes the speed that governs the fashion industry, as well as the timeless nature of the designs.

Intelligent and refined, many of the designs are also unisex and reversible. Harrer looks particularly for materials that reveal their own story to her. Producing predominately outerwear in the form of jackets and coats, Harrer eschews the catwalk, preferring to present her creations in fashion art performances that include elements of film, street art, sound art and graffiti, and often involve the audience as participants in the live act.

The 'k/white' collection of pure white outfits, spray-painted onstage, was made from a building-industry basic: a completely washable, paperlike material that retains each and every fold and crease, giving each piece its inimitable character. In logical progression, the 'k/black' collection used the same building material, only this time in black. The unique characteristic of the fabric meant that the 'k/white' collection, which began life white, ended up coloured, while the 'k/black' collection started off black but slowly faded as each scratch, crack and fold revealed the white base underneath. The customer became a participant in the creation of the garment, individualizing the clothes through wear.

The ongoing prison blanket collection is a continuation of Harrer's use of unconventional materials. The blankets, from Austrian prisons, were made by the prisoners themselves, as well as used by them. Each blanket tells the story of a prisoner's daily life through worn and faded patches and holes, with the 'Justizanstalt' prison name interwoven into the body of each design.

The reworking of the blankets into coats endows them with an entirely new and incongruent context. Remaining true to the ideals of recycling, Harrer also presented a collection of jackets, coats and dresses handcrafted from decommissioned Italian air-force parachutes. Each item retains the original seaming and authentic details, such as ripcord closures, oversized packed hoods and identifying numbers.

km/a consistently produces understated and sophisticated outerwear, using different yet equally unique base materials each season, which dictates the intricacy and details of the collection. The fashion industry has been guilty for some time now of navel-gazing. The multifaceted work of talented cross-disciplinary designers like Harrer breathes new life into an industry whose globalized operating system is no longer sustainable.

THIS COLLECTION WAS MADE
PREDOMINATELY FROM TINY SCRAPS
OF COTTON JERSEY CRAZY-STITCHED
ONTO A SINGLE JERSEY BASE.

KONDAKIS

AN ENVIRONMENTALLY AND SOCIALLY RESPONSIBLE FASHION COMPANY BASED IN KENYA, KONDAKIS CREATES A RANGE OF WOMENSWEAR FROM RECYCLED PARACHUTES, AND HANDCRAFTED ACCESSORIES FROM DEAD WOOD AND FOUND OBJECTS.

All the styles in the 'Parachute Collection' incorporate the original stitching from the parachute; some have stamps and markings intact, revealing when it was made and for whom, while all pieces joyfully celebrate the amazing structure and workmanship. KONDAKIS minimizes the environmental impact of manufacture, since the materials had already been produced for another purpose and had come to the end of that life. The parachutes remain in their original colours, ranging from snow white, through silver grey to lava orange, bush green and camouflage. They are made from 100 per cent nylon ripstop, a textile with small, strongly woven lines running through it to make it stronger and, as the name suggests, to stop it from ripping. Designs are lined with cotton for comfort against the skin.

Parachutes come in different scales and shapes, meaning that each one has to be individually cut and fashioned. Customers order directly from a small, by-appointment-only showroom in Nairobi, where they can pick a design from a sample range, customizing it if desired. Parachutes are sourced from various locations, including the military and private skydiving clubs, with most coming from the UK, the USA and Australia, although they have occasionally been bought on eBay, and, even once, from the Burning Man festival

MADE FROM DECOMMISSIONED PARACHUTES IN THEIR ORIGINAL COLOURS, THE DESIGNS ARE LINED IN COTTON FOR COMFORT.

in Nevada. At the start, sourcing the materials was one of the hardest components of designer Nike Kondakis's work, having to track down each parachute one at a time, purchasing over the internet and paying high import duties to have them shipped to Kenya. Now a network of people routinely contact her when they have parachutes ready for retirement. Kondakis also produces a collection made entirely from peace silk – silk that is produced from silkworms allowed to live their full life and eat their way out of the cocoon. Designs can be worn in multiple ways, thereby not only recycling materials, but also her own output.

Of Greek and Danish descent, Kondakis grew up in Europe, attending a number of art and design schools before joining KaosPilots in Denmark, a three-year programme in responsible entrepreneurship. Since her move to Kenya, Kondakis has set up the Lorika Foundation, a project aimed at educating Maasai girls in the Kenyan bush, and in which she invests a percentage of all sales. Kondakis is a firm believer that education is one of the strongest tools through which individuals can create change not just for themselves, but also for future generations. The Lorika Foundation is helping to prioritize Maasai girls' education, which often suffers when families have to make the hard choice of who can and who cannot go to school. Effecting positive change by example, the catchphrase for the recycled parachute collection is: 'Your mind is like a parachute, it only works when it is open.'

THE COLLECTION IS PRODUCED
LOCALLY IN KENYA UNDER
FAIR-TRADE CONDITIONS.

LU FLUX

THIS DELIGHTFULLY
LIGHT-HEARTED AND
QUIRKY WOMENSWEAR
COLLECTION IS BASED
ON BRITISH ECCENTRICITY
AND A LOVE OF TRADITIONAL
TECHNIQUES COMBINED
WITH MODERN DESIGN.

Working with complex pleating, knitting and patchwork, Lu Flux playfully combines one-off fabric finds. Working predominately with salvaged and vintage materials rescued from textile recycling plants, as much for access to the quirky undervalued fabrics they favour as for the sustainable benefit, the company also uses British-made, end-of-line materials that would otherwise go to waste.

Originally from the Isle of Wight, Lu Flux studied design at Edinburgh College of Art, before going on to assist Bernhard Willhelm in Paris. Showing at London's eco-conscious trade show Estethica, in 2010 the brand was given the Innovation Award in conjunction with the Ethical Fashion Forum, and highlighted as 'Ones to Watch' by Vauxhall Fashion Scouts. A hoarder by nature, the designer presents a collection that is a very personal expression of her look and belief in enjoying the process.

The label simply could not be anything but British – its eccentric flights of fancy are intrinsically so. The collection is the children's television programme *The Magic Roundabout* come to life in technicolour, with jackets pieced together from your grandfather's sweater and skirts made from your favourite childhood duvet. The insanity of the print and pattern mix adds

PIECES FROM THE A-LU-HA
COLLECTION: WATERFALL
MACKINTOSH (OPPOSITE) AND
LEI BLOUSE WITH SHREDDED
GRASS SKIRT (RIGHT).

to the charm of the collection, which is a dreamlike adventure, scattered with childhood memories and cultural metaphors. This is a clothing line surely made for Alice Horton, the dippy blonde from the British comedy series *The Vicar of Dibley*, who still believes in the tooth fairy, the Easter bunny and Father Christmas. It is an innocent land where colour and pattern collide with reality to brighten our waking moments, with the curler-laden head of iconic English washerwoman Nora Batty from the British sitcom *Last of the Summer Wine* as a style icon.

The repertoire of materials includes dated, unfashionable clothing items and interior textiles, mixed together Willy Wonka style, as if they have come out of the end of a crazy machine, fully formed, totally mad and completely unique. The collection features oven mittens paired with a retro floral muumuu, reimagined into a wonderfully mad scarf. This is a world where a curtain pelmet is refashioned into the trim of a jacket, and a kitsch holiday dishcloth becomes a skirt. Unfashionable items are twisted and reconfigured into idiosyncratic designs with more than a hint of humour. Lu Flux is an upturned universe where sophistication and minimalism is boring, and lunacy revered.

It is impossible not to love this collection, its naïve charm totally wins you over; whether you would wear it or not, you cannot help but smile just looking at it. The lunacy continues throughout all that Lu Flux does, with models cut and pasted into the quaint and overcrowded world of a doll's house, and designs named the 'Bricklayer Waistcoat' and the 'Chore Blouse'. The collection is infused with cultural codes and meaning, carefully cultivated over seasons, each one seeing a marked development in Flux's very personal sense of style. Aptly named collections – 'A-Lu-Ha', 'Everything But the Kitchen Sink' – can be found at a range of retailers from London to Australia to Japan.

DUST COAT, CHORE BLOUSE
AND TRICKLE MITTENS (OPPOSITE),
CARPET JACKET AND POWDER
ROOM SKIRT (LEFT), ALL FROM
THE EVERYTHING BUT THE
KITCHEN SINK COLLECTION.

MAYER PEACE COLLECTION

BERLIN-BASED LABEL
MAYER PEACE COLLECTION,
FOUNDED IN 2004, FUSES
FASHION AND CHARITY,
TRANSFORMING RECYCLED
MATERIALS.

ABOVE: LINEN AND HEMP JACKET
PRODUCED FROM VINTAGE GERMAN
FLOUR SACKS AND FEATURING THE
ORIGINAL GRAPHIC IDENTIFICATION
OF THE FARM AND THE FARMER.

OPPOSITE: JACKET MADE ENTIRELY
FROM UPCYCLED AND PATCHWORKED
DENIM JEANS, INCLUDING POCKETS,
TABS AND WAISTBANDS.

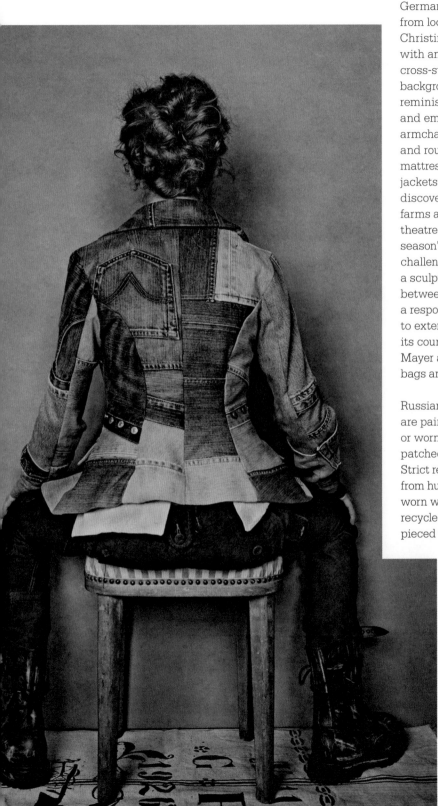

Growing up in the Black Forest in the south of Germany and playing games around the grain sacks from local mills in her grandfather's barn, founder Christine Mayer remains true to her origins. Working with antique flour sacks from the mid-1850s; folkloric cross-stitched embroidery patterns on striking white backgrounds with scarlet hand-stitched monograms reminiscent of country table linen; richly embellished and embroidered curtains; a mother's decorative armchair protector; a grandmother's delicate trousseau; and rough, hard-wearing handwoven linens and mattress ticking, Mayer beautifully handcrafts tailored jackets and coordinating separates. She relishes discovering new materials from traditional Bavarian farms and mills, antique dealers, flea markets and theatre inventory clearances, which inform each season's direction and signify a new and exciting challenge. Mayer sees her role much like that of a sculptor, establishing a form of communication between the material and the creator, and with a responsibility to set the material's story free and to extend its life, while letting her creativity run its course. Always fascinated by historic materials, Mayer also sources military textiles, such as marine bags and armed forces capes from across Europe.

Russian-army or Napoleonic-style military jackets are paired with Provençal-style tablecloth skirts or worn over urban khaki low-crotched and multi-patched-and-pocketed trousers with jackboots. Strict retro military-cut jackets feature sleeves crafted from humble milkmaid cross-stitched aprons and are worn with asymmetric tea-towel skirts. Patchworked recycled denim jeans, inventively reimagined from pieced waistbands, pockets and yokes, form entirely

THE ORNAMENTAL JACKET
(OPPOSITE) FEATURES HEAVY
DOMESTIC EMBROIDERY ON THE
SLEEVES, WHILE THE UTILITARIAN
STYLING OF THE BLOUSE AND
SKIRT (BELOW) HAS SIMPLE
CONTRASTING WOVEN EDGING.

new feminine pieces, strictly tailored jackets and slouchy low-slung trousers. Mayer takes wonderful advantage of the myriad shades in washed and worn denim to create variations in tone and colour within a single piece. The collection also incorporates combat military pieces with multiple pockets and tabs, bringing a decidedly urban feel to balance out the pretty white linen coordinates. With a focus on expressing contrast within her collections, Mayer merges robust looks, elaborate embroidery, feminine fits and exceptional cuts, forming a unique look and making a harmonious and poetic unity.

With a background in fur production, Mayer learned an appreciation of patching and cutting materials and piecing them back together through the complex process of slashing and re-sewing skins. Developed step by step according to Mayer's innate sense of where each piece belongs, each design is hand cut and placed, working directly on the mannequin. The highly decorative pieces are placed first, followed by the leftovers, all moulded into sharp cuts and feminine curves. The unique nature of each of the materials means that there are no actual patterns, while the individual moulding leads to a very feminine fit and line. Inspired by history, in particular nineteenth- and twentieth-century theatrical costumes, Mayer is also influenced by global patterns and embroideries.

A portion of profits from all MAYER Peace Collection designs benefits children's charity projects in Nepal and India. With a trace of spirituality woven in between the threads of the material, every garment provides strength and gives the wearer the impetus to move beyond her own horizons.

MILCH

AUSTRIAN LABEL
MILCH DESIGNS A WOMEN'S
COLLECTION PRODUCED FROM
UPCYCLED, CLASSIC MENSWEAR
TROUSERS AND SHIRTS.

MEN'S SUIT TROUSERS, TURNED
UPSIDE DOWN WITH THE WAISTBAND
AT THE HEM, ARE UPCYCLED
TO CREATE DRESSES AND SKIRTS.

Known as the 'trouser dress collection', timeless men's fashion is hijacked and subverted, transformed into thoroughly modern pieces for women. There is a quirky playfulness to the urban look, with turned-up men's trousers reconfigured into body-skimming shift dresses, with waistbands forming a pulled-in hemline. A man's pinstripe cotton shirt becomes a wrapped and tied skirt with the sleeves forming a bow. A pretty cap-sleeved peasant top with a ruched neckline is made from a man's crisp white cotton shirt. A lovely and intriguing counterbalance is created through the reinterpretation of masculine, tailored wool trousers and cotton shirts into feminine shift dresses and skirt trousers. The collection is completed by a range of quirky bags and hats made entirely from the back-pocket details of men's trousers.

Established in 1998 by fashion designer Cloed Priscilla Baumgartner, MILCH works with only the best discarded menswear, sourced and produced in Vienna in an ethical and sustainable manner. Environmental and social considerations are taken into account throughout production, with all work undertaken in fair-trade conditions. All second-hand clothing is carefully washed in a chain of launderettes known as Green Clean, which use only Ecover washing detergents and softeners and carefully weigh washloads to ensure no unnecessary water is used. A team of talented seamstresses and homeworkers in the Vienna area individually sew all MILCH designs, making the product truly locally produced and, therefore, with a small carbon footprint.

MILCH only works with natural fibres and donations from recycled clothing agencies such as Volkshilfe Box in Vienna, from which it receives trousers and shirts by the kilo. Applying upcycling techniques to reuse leftovers in new ways, MILCH diverts a portion of materials from the mountain of textile waste destined for landfill. Making precious and subversive things out of civilization's garbage, and bringing them back to life through recycling, is a source of great satisfaction to Baumgartner. The restriction and repetition of the styling and materials drive her creativity, allowing her to focus on clever use of details, such as buttons, plackets and pockets. Baumgartner relishes the appropriation of men's work uniforms, turning our cultural understanding of the materials on its head by transforming them into unique womenswear. The general uniformity of styling in menswear means that MILCH is able to cut multiple garments at once in layered batches and still achieve individuality, an important factor when selling designs across five European countries and more than 25 stores.

Baumgartner is also the founder of Vienna's largest fashion fair, Modepalast, and curates her own eco-design showroom named YPPIG. MILCH has won several awards in the field of sustainability and innovation, reaffirming it as a well-respected and established brand in eco-fashion.

THE CLASSIC FLAT CAP (ABOVE)
IS FASHIONED FROM A BACK POCKET
FROM MEN'S SUIT TROUSERS, WHILE
THE DRESS (OPPOSITE) IS MADE ENTIRELY
FROM MEN'S SHIRT COLLARS.

TRUE DENIM CONNOISSEURS, NUDIE LOVE
JEANS WITH A PASSION, OFFERING A LIFESTYLE
AND A CONCEPT FUELLED BY THE TRADITIONS
OF THE FABRIC ITSELF.

DESIGNERS WORKING WITH USED MATERIALS

NUDIE JEANS

FINDING A COMPANY THAT TACKLES THE MANY AND COMPLEX ISSUES INVOLVED IN DENIM-JEAN MANUFACTURE IS LIKE LOOKING FOR A NEEDLE IN A HAYSTACK: FEW ATTEMPT IT AND EVEN FEWER SUCCEED.

Nudie Jeans is one of the few doing it right. Denim jeans are the most common item found in most people's wardrobes, but they are also one of the dirtiest and most wasteful products to manufacture. Conventional cotton crops use approximately a quarter of the world's insecticides, and ten per cent of the world's pesticides,[1] causing pesticide poisoning in countless agricultural workers around the world.[2] It also uses vast quantities of water to grow, to wash and to dye the denim, and then again to distress it, not to mention post-purchase laundering. Those attractive worn patches that make your jeans appear lived in before you even buy them are too often achieved from sandblasting, a process that has caused silicosis in more than 40 operators in Turkey alone.[3]

Nudie Jeans cares about its jeans – the way they are produced, from both a human and an environmental perspective. When they are worn out it repairs them; it reuses them and, finally, it recycles them. The label does not see a trade-off between profit and people, or manufacture and environmental responsibility, all of which play a major role in its supplier relationships. Most of Nudie's jeans are made from organic cotton, certified by the Global Organic Textile Standard (GOTS), and the entire production chain, from cotton to jeans, is certified. The company is a member of

OLD, WORN-OUT NUDIE JEANS ARE
CUT INTO PIECES AND RECYCLED
INTO NEW DENIM CLOTHING.

the Textile Exchange, a non-profit organization that supports the farming and trading of organically grown cotton, and also of the Fair Wear Foundation, an independent, non-profit organization that strives to improve working conditions in the textile industry. Nudie Jeans also supports Amnesty International through T-shirt sales, and has generated in excess of 350,000 euros for its cause to date.

Firm believers in the notions of reduce, reuse and recycle, Nudie repairs jeans purchased from the company for free in its stores. The label also works with recycled cotton, producing multiple styles made exclusively from worn-out jeans. Unwanted jeans are shredded and mixed in with leftover denim cuttings from production. The shredded textiles are milled down to a cotton pulp, then spun into new yarn, which is used to create new denim fabric. Nudie also created the 'Recycle Denim Maniacs' programme, through which textile students are invited to create new conceptual fashion designs from old Nudie jeans.

True denim lovers, Nudie Jeans has a passion for its craft and an undying respect for the textile jeans are made from. It sees jeans as culturally iconic, unique garments that react to your lifestyle and reflect your personal character through wear. For the label, denim is a living material, which even bleeds, and whose beauty increases with age and wear. Not interested in fads and fashion, Nudie's inspiration is found far from the catwalk in the worlds of music and film, as well as in the history of denim, the Swedish worker culture and the melting pot of modern Scandinavia.

1 Taken from information published online at:
  www.ota.com/organic/environment/cotton_environment.html
2 Taken from information published online at:
  www.ejfoundation.org/page324.html
3 Taken from information published online at:
  www.cleanclothes.org/resources/ccc/working-conditions/
  deadly-denim-sandblasting-in-the-bangladesh-garment-industry

ODETTE PICAUD

A JEWELRY AND CLOTHING COLLECTION, ODETTE PICAUD ACTS AS A CONDUIT FOR AN ESOTERIC JOURNEY INTO THE PAST, THROUGH ADORNMENT, MEMORY, CONNECTION AND HISTORY, AS SEEN THROUGH THE EYES OF THE FICTIONAL AND HISTORIC FIGURE OF ODETTE.

Designer Fanny Crenn is based in Brittany, France, while Odette, who operates as her muse, lives in Crenn's heart and her mind. Crenn's jewelry and clothing have the appearance of a particularly eclectic designer's mood board or an artist's journal filled with mementos and visual memories from the past. The mix of items includes old photos, leather gloves, battered and beaten dominoes, crosses and old lace. Her clothing is a flight of fancy that would not look out of place adorning Titania, queen of the fairies, in Shakespeare's *A Midsummer Night's Dream*.

Sourcing her materials from flea markets, second-hand stores and attic sales, Crenn references the Emmaus Movement, the collective fight against all forms of exclusion, started by the French Catholic priest Henri Marie Joseph Groues, otherwise known as Abbé Pierre. The charity that continues in his name is often the source of Crenn's ephemera, which becomes her jewelry and clothing line. Only using vintage finds, Crenn has a particular penchant for gloves, leather, rosaries, rabbit droppings, textile scraps, photos, feathers, rodent bones, pearls, lace, medals, buttons and toys! That diverse list acts as the source material for every collection, while her creative process imbues the faded items with a dark undertone, as if conceived for the central character of Tim Burton's *Corpse Bride*.

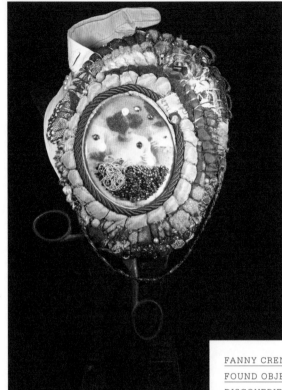

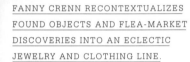

DESIGNERS WORKING WITH USED MATERIALS

Crenn's affair with artifacts from the past and their recontextualization into ethereal jewelry, clothing, dolls and wall ornaments started during her art studies at the University of Rennes in 2004. She began working with the past and preserving memories, producing a collection of old and strange clothes made from blankets for her end-of-year diploma exhibition. There, in the relics from the past reinterpreted for the present, appeared Odette, making her way into Crenn's every design in some way, shape or form, like a familiar family ghost come home.

The inspiration for Odette Picaud came from a found suitcase in a recycling centre, full of old papers and family pictures, labelled 'Mum's things'. Mum was called Odette Picaud, a name and face that Crenn immediately connected with. Odette Picaud's memories have formed the basis of the collection of work that is Odette Picaud ever since. Each item is unique and handmade, assembled and sewn in Crenn's western France showroom in the countryside of Brittany. Often thought of as strange and eccentric, Crenn's work is nevertheless a tangible connection to the past, with each creation acting as a visual and tactile memory and a conduit to times gone by.

The birth of Crenn's son in 2004 marked the start of the collection, originally called 'Les Bijoux d'Odette'. The more recent birth of her daughter heralded a new creative connection to the past, with the introduction of strange and curious dolls in the same vein as the jewels and the clothing. These odd and slightly freaky creatures with scissor heads and hand-sewn bodies border somewhere between fantasy and fiction, with much in common with ancient African fertility figures – hauntingly attractive and viscerally repulsive at the same time.

OTRA (ON THE ROAD AGAIN)

THE COMPANY WAS FOUNDED BY FRENCH PARTNERS JULIE FERRERO AND GUILLAUME DARNAJOU AFTER TAKING TO THE ROAD IN TOULON, FRANCE, AND ENDING UP IN MONTREAL, CANADA.

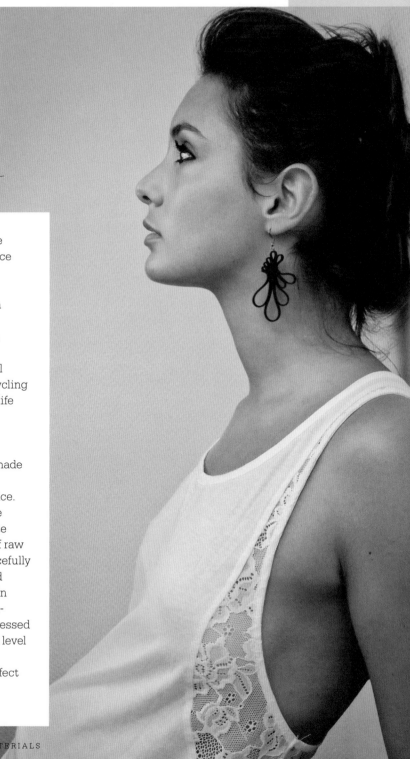

The pair's travels took them from their first degree in product design at La Grande Tourrache in France to their second degree in industrial design at the University of Montreal. Soon thereafter, the Otra workshop came into being, inspired by a common desire to direct their work toward sustainability. Concerned with society's over-consumption, Otra nurtures a deep-rooted passion for environmental design, forging new design practices and material use. Re-evaluating waste, Otra builds on the upcycling movement by creating a second more purposeful life from undervalued materials.

The Otra workshop produces an intricate and futuristic-looking jewelry collection, entirely handmade from bicycle tyre inner tubes. The name of the company refers, of course, to their material of choice. Bicycle culture in Montreal is plentiful and bicycle inner tubes are not usually recyclable. The delicate filigreed style of Otra's jewelry belies the choice of raw materials, with tiny bands of jet-black rubber gracefully undulating and coiled into earrings, pendants and cuffs. Designs are gently feathered with micro-thin slivers of rubber, or appear to be inspired by moth-eaten cocoons given new futuristic form and expressed with an eerie exactness. The material allows for a level of exactitude, dimension and delicacy that is not easily imagined. This is often set off to graphic effect by incorporating the printing on the tyre itself.

ALL OF OTRA'S INTRICATE
DESIGNS ARE INDIVIDUALLY
CUT BY HAND, GIVING EACH
PIECE A VALUE INVESTED
BY THE LABOUR RATHER
THAN THE RAW MATERIAL.

DESIGNERS WORKING WITH USED MATERIALS

TRA JEWELRY IS MADE ENTIRELY
ROM LOCALLY SOURCED BICYCLE TYRE
JNER TUBES, AND ASSEMBLED WITHOUT
HE AID OF PAINT, SOLVENT OR GLUE.

Eschewing the use of lasers and dyes, every item is carefully and accurately hand cut, while the raw materials are reclaimed from neighbouring bicycle-repair stores. Materials are smothered in skin cream to intensify and perfect the depth of colour, and are assembled using only studs, pins and hooks, without the use of any paint, solvent or glue. The tyres are even used to make the thread for the necklaces by cutting them into slivers. The reused materials imbue the designs with a strong and unique character, all the more intriguing because of the apparent paradox between worn-out bicycle tyres and the dangling, delicate earrings. It is Ferrero and Darnajou's intent to highlight the paradox between the lack of worth in the discarded, recycled materials and the inherent value of the finished product, with the value coming from their manual work and artistry.

Otra's product range is broader than simply jewelry, also including a geometric range of self-assembly reversible lampshades, polymorphic by design, and produced from recycled plastic advertisement posters, all scavenged from the Montreal subway system.

RAGGEDY

BASED IN WALES,
RAGGEDY CREATES RECYCLED
WOMEN'S CLOTHING BY COMBINING
KNITWEAR, TWEEDS, LINENS AND
COTTON INTO NEW INCARNATIONS
OF QUIRKY COUTURE.

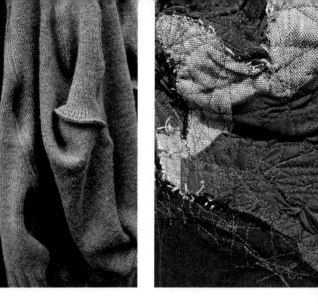

Designs are raw and playful in nature, with more than a passing resemblance to a romanticized Oliver Twist or a Victorian noblewoman fallen on hard times. The work is a sort of extreme version of make do and mend, as viewed through an idealized Victorian London, or Wales come to that. Raggedy uses a wonderful mix of knobbly tweeds, houndstooth and heathered wools crazily patched and pieced together into shrunken versions of turn-of-the-century men's waistcoats and women's riding jackets. These are worn with jauntily hitched and ruched petticoat-style skirts with flounces, lacing and frills, all cobbled together into a pleasing deconstructed whole. Using the tiniest scraps and rags of textile remnants, Raggedy reimagines corsets and bustles in vibrant colour combinations, accentuating tiny waists and full busts to dramatic effect. This is artwork as clothing, patchwork for the fashionista, but very wearable, albeit with a vintage tongue-in-cheek lunacy.

Designer Hayley Tresize sees the history in everything she cuts, working with that vision to help her reimagine her designs, and loving the idea of an old man's tweed coat reborn as a funky dress for a young woman. Some styles sport crazy overlays of yarn and stitching or bold contrasting zigzag stitches, which Tresize refers to as 'scribble stitch', giving textiles the appearance of three-dimensional topographical maps or aerial photographs via satellite. Scribble stitch creates a fabric from scratch by stitching tiny scraps of material on top of each other to form a spider's web of textiles. She begins by matching materials, but goes on to mismatch colours

TINY SCRAPS OF KNITWEAR, TWEED, LINEN AND COTTON ARE BOUND TOGETHER AND REINCARNATED WITH RAGGEDY'S SIGNATURE INTRICATE 'SCRIBBLE STITCH'.

and textures. Tresize brazenly cuts by eye, using only her imagination as a guide, and never with the aid of a pattern. Her aim is to cut without fear, viewing the often unexpected results as the means of producing new designs.

Recycling and sustainability form the underlying ethos of all Tresize's work. She raises awareness of recycling through her designs, but also by running recycled-clothing workshops at colleges and for the public, where sewing skills and design ideas are shared, empowering people on a personal level and enabling them to do it for themselves. Self-taught, Tresize attended art college to study sculpture, where she focused on textures, shapes and space. She began designing clothes in her teenage years through a desire to dress differently, mashing her favourite things into one outfit, safety-pinning things together to create a look. Later, her love of individuality, merged with her belief in sustainability, led her to found Raggedy.

Living in Wales in a beautiful antique yurt, Tresize is close to nature, while still in touch with the modern world through the internet. She likes to question freedom through her clothes, helping women to express their individuality and to dress as they desire without fear or judgement.

SAISEI

IN JAPANESE, *SAISEI*
MEANS REBIRTH AND RECOVERY,
THE PHILOSOPHY
UPON WHICH THE COMPANY
NAME IS FOUNDED.

Collections are based on forgotten fabrics, brought back to life through craftsmanship, and combined with contemporary style. Saisei's tireless research has resulted in its broad-based textile usage, which includes old military kits, tents, army fabrics and ship sails, each one carrying a heroic history and an almost forgotten story, both of which are revived through redesign. Disassembled, reassembled and reinvented, these scraps of textiles are given new life through skillful Italian manufacture. The bags have clean, simple, almost Zen-like lines, turning the focus on to the material choice and use. Contrasting interior linings in retro florals, Highland tartan and French toile de Jouy strengthen the minimal exterior. Volume is key to the label; Saisei sees its bags as containers for the customer's world, who, in turn, personalizes his or her creation through use. In spite of the bags' strong characters and identities, they are nevertheless genderless.

Bologna-based founder and designer Georgia Palmirani uses her interior- and architectural-design background to great effect through the development of her bags. Influenced by her studies in the rich artistic cultures of Madrid and Florence, she developed her love of decor, architecture and interior design. Her natural curiosity and love of experimentation led her to start ESERCIZIDISTILE (exercises of style), based on the concept of reusing recycled fabrics and revaluing the Italian textile tradition. This, in turn, brought about the development of Saisei.

Rooted in material and process research, the Saisei collections always grow out of the material: its destination, its renewal and its evolution. The search for and revival of forgotten fabrics is a constant, with each piece carrying its unique story. Saisei also develops experimental dyeing techniques and finishes. One of these is an exclusive waxing process, which highlights the original nature and tone of the fabric finds.

The collection incorporates a deliberately simple line of shopping bags, backpacks, messenger bags and totes, featuring utilitarian army webbing and clean leather straps and handles. Different material themes make up the various lines. 'Mash' is assembled from pieces of old Italian army tents, including the writing, studding and straps, with worn and faded corners that emphasize the depth and richness of colour. 'Vespucci' is a line of bags made exclusively from the recovered hemp sails of the Vespucci School ships. Dyed and waxed hemp is painted by hand with strokes of contrasting acrylic paint. The well-used sails are richly embellished with deep tonal dyes and highlighted by the light sheen of a waxed surface, similar in character and strength to the iconic Barbour hunting jacket. The authenticity of the materials, combined with the sophisticated and understated designs, make for a beautifully weathered line of utilitarian bags.

SAISEI BAGS ARE CONSTRUCTED OUT
OF VINTAGE MILITARY KITS, TENTS,
ARMY WEBBING AND SHIP SAILS, COMBINED
WITH EXPERIMENTAL DYEING TECHNIQUES
AND FINISHES.

THE ECLECTIC AND AVANT-GARDE
COLLECTION OF SCHMIDT TAKAHASHI
IS ENTIRELY ASSEMBLED FROM
CLOTHING DONATIONS.

SCHMIDT TAKAHASHI

AS THE NAME SUGGESTS,
THERE IS A HYBRID
ASIAN–GERMAN AESTHETIC
TO THIS COLLECTION OF
WOMENS- AND MENSWEAR,
WHICH ACHIEVES A SORT OF
DISCORDANT SYMMETRY.

Schmidt Takahashi is a Berlin-based label that specializes in upcycled, restyled and redesigned clothing. Eugenie Schmidt, born in Tajikistan and educated in Berlin and at the renowned Royal Academy of Fine Arts in Antwerp, Belgium, and Mariko Takahashi, born and educated in Tokyo and Berlin, make up the label. Their unique partnership creates a wonderfully eclectic and avant-garde look, incorporating incongruous layered combinations to form a harmonious whole.

Working with clothing donations, Schmidt Takahashi strips down each item, only to reassemble it in an entirely new configuration. Designs are rarely predetermined; each style evolves naturally to create a hybrid aesthetic. The designers' approach is immediate and intuitive, resulting in seemingly incompatible pairings, such as a trench coat with a down jacket; a classic men's chequered jacket with a woman's fur coat; or a silk shirt transformed into a summer dress and pulled in with a heavy-knit cardigan belt. The brand revels in its unconventional cuts, proportions, fabric and garment combinations. But, despite the diversity of materials and styles, Schmidt Takahashi pays particular attention to the final harmony of the design. Each piece is lined with the highest quality pure silk to improve comfort and appearance, but also to add to the longevity of its new life.

'Wiederbelebungsmassnahmen' or 'Identity Swapping' is the name of the designers' project, which seeks to value, track and communicate the history of each item that goes into their redesigned collection. The project furnishes the donor of the clothing with a unique identification number to track the item's future life. Garments are donated in a special container, which accompanies the partners on their travels. Schmidt and Takahashi believe that garments carry with them a heritage and multiple stories absorbed through wear; the clothing provides the wearer with an external skin that stores information unique to its owner.

Each donated item is carefully washed and ironed and assigned an identification number unique to the former owner. The colour, material and style are catalogued and archival photographs taken. This information is then saved as a Quick Response code (a type of two-dimensional barcode, which can be read with any QR code reader, available on most smartphones as an application download). The QR code simultaneously acts as a label and a history recorder. It also means that the garment's history may be accessed at any time, or its new life tracked.

THE UNEXPECTED PAIRING OF INCONGRUOUS LAYERED COMBINATIONS IS SCHMIDT TAKAHASHI'S SIGNATURE.

SILENT PEOPLE

ITALIAN LABEL SILENT PEOPLE
ARTFULLY PRODUCES
A COLLECTION OF BAGS AND
ACCESSORIES FROM A DIVERSE
RANGE OF HERITAGE-LADEN,
VINTAGE AND RECYCLED
MATERIALS.

ONE-OF-A-KIND SILENT PEOPLE
BAGS ARE INDIVIDUALLY CRAFTED
WITH TRUE ITALIAN ARTISANSHIP.

Putting an entirely new twist on heritage, the label's unique remade collection of bags has an authentic, avant-garde look, achieved through an inventive use of myriad worn and discarded materials, ranging from gas-mask cases to Italian army inflatable mattresses. Based in Bologna, Italy, Franco Armilla and Filippo Biancoli piece together each bag one at a time to create pieces that sing of bequeathed and inherited tradition, myth and history, from upcycled luxury brands, authentic workwear and military paraphernalia. They work with iconic and classic items, including traditional trench coats by Burberry with their emblematic checked linings, shiny Italian Moncler padded jackets and the symbolic British twinset-and-pearls favourite: Barbour waxed-cotton jackets.

The designers cut, piece, rework and remodel. Scraps, remnants and pieces of global brand heritage are reinvented as bags, leaving just a hint of their past life, enough to haunt the present. Historically rich materials such as Italian army Red Cross field tents from World War II feature in the collection. The duo match 1970s leather biker jackets with horse bridle handles, while 1940s Austrian military spats are used as fastenings, or 1930s German police jackets are paired with military belt handles – all lined with Italian army hemp mattress covers. This inventive balancing act is achieved through the careful patching and matching of materials to bring a well-loved quality to the bags (even before they are purchased and used).

Armilla feeds his passion by working with and discovering new materials and forgotten techniques, based on true Italian artisanal tradition. He reveals each material's hidden narrative, releasing and expressing its character. Biancoli revels in the vintage nature of the materials and the unique objects they work with, enjoying matching the past with the present, and the task of harmonizing the varied stories each one brings to the item as a whole.

Each bag bears its own individual name, such as Motika, Demetra and Alcatraz. The array of non-traditional and inimitable history-infused items that make their way into a Silent People bag is truly dizzying. The permutations are as endless as the designers' imaginations, making this an adventurous and artistic line of bags produced in the Italian tradition of luxury handmade leather goods.

THE UNIQUE COLLECTION OF BAGS IS HANDCRAFTED FROM AUTHENTIC DISCARDED MATERIALS SUCH AS GAS-MASK CASES AND INFLATABLE MATTRESSES FROM THE ITALIAN ARMY.

SYLWIA ROCHALA

WARSAW-BASED DESIGNER
SYLWIA ROCHALA INCORPORATES
RECYCLED MATERIALS INTO ALL
OF HER COLLECTIONS.

THE SHEER AND OPAQUE FABRIC COMBINATIONS OF THE X-RAY COLLECTION ECHO THE DELICATE NATURE OF HUMAN SKIN.

With a history of developmental research into recycled material use, Rochala expands and varies her recycling and upcycling techniques each season. Her first collection, 'Shaman' in 2010, used men's old silk shirts, ripping them into strips and hand-knotting them together to form dresses. Pieces mimicked the couture fluting technique of laying bias-cut strips on a sheer background to allow for subtle and sensual peeks of flesh between the gaps – only achieved with a punk aesthetic. The results were a modern vixenish take on an ancient Egyptian mummy, or, perhaps, a sensual bride of Frankenstein, and were paired with patchworked leggings created from pieced jersey blouses.

For her second season, Rochala used unravelled yarn from second-hand sweaters to produce a lacey collection of holey hand knits, entitled 'Prospero'. A development of both the bias-cut shirt knotting and the upcycled sweater yarn projects constituted the basis of the following collection, called 'Snag'. True to its name, 'Snag' focused on roughness and obscurity through pulls and breaks in the fabric base, incorporating tears and patches, and purposely imperfect knits that were either too short or too long.

The 'Boro' collection was inspired by the ancient Japanese garments of the same name, pieced together by the impoverished from reused and recycled indigo cotton rags. Working with men's used silk and denim shirts as base materials, the fabric was bleached to mimic Japanese Shibori dye techniques, only in reverse. She made circle skirts and patched peplum jackets, which were coordinated with pale, soft feminine skirts and dresses to offset the dark tones of the denim. She also incorporated her trademark banding and wrapping technique into opaque and sheer monochromatic leggings, tightly wrapped tops and micro miniskirts.

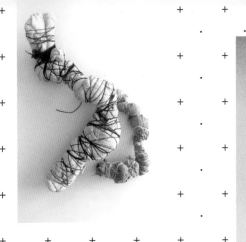

Pale silk was the main material in the 'X-Ray' collection, in which tie-dyed silk shirts in soft coral, blush and lavender tones created a light, airy, semi-sheer range of wafting, layered dresses. Cut-outs, peepholes and asymmetrical layers played with colour and shape and sheer and opaque qualities. Based around the idea of the human body as a thin transparent skin holding within it the solidity and function of our organs, the collection depicted and revealed the body as viewed in science and art, through the use of layers of translucent fabric suggesting X-rays.

Rochala is known for her provocative individuality and respect for fabrics. She nobly recycles textiles, creating the new by ripping the old out of context. Colour, concept and fabric fuel her imaginative processes, and all her collections are produced in Poland. Sylwia Rochala presents her iconic collection off-schedule during Polish and Berlin fashion weeks.

SHREDDED MEN'S SILK SHIRTS, DELICATELY LAYERED AND KNOTTED TOGETHER, CREATE EXQUISITE PIECES IN THE SHAMANI TRADITION.

LATE 19TH-CENTURY
JAPANESE BORO TEXTILES
INSPIRED ROCHALA'S
USE OF SHIBORI DYEING
TECHNIQUES IN REVERSE.

TAMARA FOGLE

COMBINING A UNIQUE RANGE OF ANTIQUE TEXTILES AND LEATHERS, TAMARA FOGLE HAND MAKES MODERN TIMELESS BAGS, TOTES AND PURSES IN FAMILY-RUN WORKSHOPS IN NOTTING HILL, LONDON.

The choice of material is central to Fogle's approach, and includes upcycled German flour sacks, Hungarian grain sacks, French mattress ticking, canvas military tents and hand-stitched quilts from Pakistan. Aided by her background in antiques and interior styling, Fogle is inspired by heritage, quality and authenticity. Each bag is unique, featuring materials ranging in age from the 1830s to the 1940s, some in perfect condition, while others show hand-stitched repairs and darning, telling their personal narratives through the stains and patches of a past life.

The materials Fogle uses have had a lifetime of service and have a story to tell. Designed to take a beating, antique German flour sacks dating from the 1830s to the 1930s form the base material of her iconic collection. Produced from 100 per cent linen, the thick heavy twill weave features the farmer's name, the location of his farm and the year the sacks were used in black Gothic typography, sometimes clearly legible, other times beautifully faded and worn. The age and original use of these sacks means they are often heavily distressed, featuring marks and repairs that enhance their inimitable beauty and history, while retaining the strength and vibrancy of the material.

Hungarian grain sacks, dating from 1910 to the 1920s, are stunningly aged and distressed. Made from coarse, 100 per cent flax linen, they sport simple red or blue

DESIGNERS WORKING WITH USED MATERIALS

stripe combinations, each one distinct to an individual farmer. Bags made from antique French mattress ticking, dating from the mid-1800s, are distinguished by brilliant graduating colour combinations within each striped band, as well as a difference in tone from one stripe to the next. Bolder stripes, dating from the 1950s onward, incorporate a striking array of vivid hues, including bright coral, deep teal and kingfisher blue. Antique French linen is also used, in varying shades of white and oatmeal, and in uneven and smooth textures. Vintage canvas military tent fabric, dating from the 1940s, features wonderful muted tones of olive through brown with a slightly crushed appearance, not dissimilar to a used paper bag. Old hand-stitched quilts from India and Pakistan, made from 100 per cent cotton, with distinct patterns, weaves and prints, date from the 1930s to the 1970s, and inject the collection with a vibrancy of colour through their distinct patterns, prints and unusual combinations.

Water-based aniline-finished leather hides are used for the highly polished handles, patches and bases of the bags, making an effective contrast to the aged and faded material on the body of the pieces. Soft aniline-finished hides use fewer chemicals in the tanning process than most other leathers, making them kinder to the environment. The method also gives a more transparent finish, showing the natural markings and scars on the skin, intensifying their individual character and bridging the gap between the distressed materials that form the body of the bag. Bags and purses are finished and complemented by antique brass frames, closures and studs, featuring Fogle's signature leather barrel closure.

Established in 2007, Tamara Fogle prides itself on its fine quality British production. Fabrics are reused primarily for their aesthetic qualities, but also create a smaller carbon footprint and less waste, as well as diverting materials from landfill. Through her production choices, Fogle helps to bring ethical fashion to the mainstream by not setting herself apart from the industry and by showcasing her collection alongside the regular schedules.

VEGETABLE-TANNED BRIDLE LEATHERS ARE USED FOR STRAPS AND HANDLES, WITH VINTAGE KATHA QUILTS AND ANTIQUE FRENCH MATTRESS TICKING FORMING THE BODY OF THE BAG.

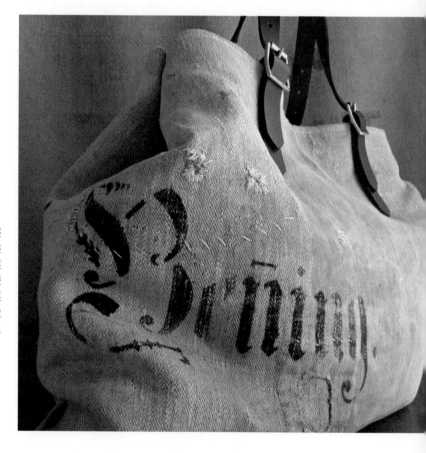

THE BEA PROJECT

A FINE-ART AND FASHION
MIXED-MEDIA ART HOUSE,
THE BEA PROJECT
IS THE BRAINCHILD
OF KATRINA BEA.

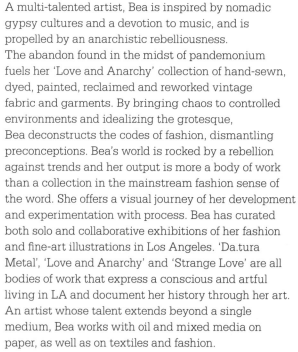

A multi-talented artist, Bea is inspired by nomadic gypsy cultures and a devotion to music, and is propelled by an anarchistic rebelliousness.
The abandon found in the midst of pandemonium fuels her 'Love and Anarchy' collection of hand-sewn, dyed, painted, reclaimed and reworked vintage fabric and garments. By bringing chaos to controlled environments and idealizing the grotesque, Bea deconstructs the codes of fashion, dismantling preconceptions. Bea's world is rocked by a rebellion against trends and her output is more a body of work than a collection in the mainstream fashion sense of the word. She offers a visual journey of her development and experimentation with process. Bea has curated both solo and collaborative exhibitions of her fashion and fine-art illustrations in Los Angeles. 'Da.tura Metal', 'Love and Anarchy' and 'Strange Love' are all bodies of work that express a conscious and artful living in LA and document her history through her art. An artist whose talent extends beyond a single medium, Bea works with oil and mixed media on paper, as well as on textiles and fashion.

'Love and Anarchy' runs the gamut from girly, vintage and sweet with naïve sexual undertones to a full-on deconstructed punk, hard-rock and grunge mélange. Fabrics and garments are rich with detail and texture, and often revolutionary. Bea appears to be the archetypal artist—creative, adept at expressing herself in many media, seeing no boundaries and fusing fashion and fine art. Her wearable art incorporates a total of 33 handmade painted and dyed outfits, with an additional 100 screen-printed dresses and T-shirts and a plethora of necklaces and utility belts, making for a post-apocalyptic look.

DECONSTRUCTED CLOTHING IS USED AS A METAPHOR TO DISMANTLE PERCEPTIONS.

The body of work is the culmination of over seven months of intensive labour, with some textiles dyed, re-dyed and bleached as many as three times, and others painted, burned and sun bleached to achieve the desired final effect. Textiles are sourced from stripped and destroyed vintage and unwanted current clothing, as well as from bolts of antique fabrics.

Video montages augment and document Bea's work, giving an entertaining and visual overview of the projects. She is an artist who uses clothes as a means of expression, exhibiting them as installations, with the flashing still and video photography showcasing the many steps involved in the creation of the collections. The images were shot by partner Jeremy Kenyon Lockyer Corbell with a sepia-toned, retro approach. The videos outline the painting, dyeing and sewing processes that Bea undertakes in the creation of her artwork and her collection, all suitably set to a grunge-rock soundtrack. The installations are the physical manifestation of many years of collaborative love, life and work for the pair. One of the things that sets Bea's work apart from that of other designers using recycled and upcycled materials is her urban, grunge, rebellious stance. She is quite unique in the industry, unconcerned with others' interpretations of fashion; she is a true artist, employing upcycled garments and process-laden textiles as her medium of expression.

EACH PIECE IN KATRINA BEA'S
FINE-ART APPAREL LINE
IS HAND-SEWN, DYED AND
PAINTED FROM RECLAIMED
AND VINTAGE MATERIALS.

TRASHED COUTURE

THIS UK LABEL IS AN ECO-FASHION COLLECTION, SPECIALIZING IN UPCYCLING SECOND-HAND DENIM.

The sexy, body-conscious, street couture brand upcycles common denim jeans into micro shorts, sexy cropped halterneck tops and pencil-slim skirts, with more than a touch of deconstruction. Entire dresses are pieced together from jean waistbands, pockets and belt tabs, replete with rivets and buttonholes as proof of authenticity as well as design features. Epaulettes and shrugs are constructed from the tiniest of leftover scraps to exuberant and dramatic effect. The inventive collection capitalizes on every remnant with daring bravado and just a touch of exhibitionism. Inspired by the sartorial attitude of the British punk-rock scene of the 1970s and 1980s, designer Sara Li-Chou Han also channels the avant-garde Antwerp deconstructionist fashion approach of the 1990s into her thoroughly modern urban designs.

Second-hand garments are sourced from vintage markets and local charity shops, often using stock that would otherwise be destined for landfill. Finding a creative solution to the problem of textile waste inspires Han's work; she attempts to answer the question of whether fashion can clean up waste, create unique styles and provide a sustainable alternative to high-street clothing. As a designer, Han is fully committed to an exploration of ethical and sustainable production and sourcing methods. Once the raw material has been sourced, the denim is cleaned using only sustainable products. At the studio in Manchester, denim jeans are carefully

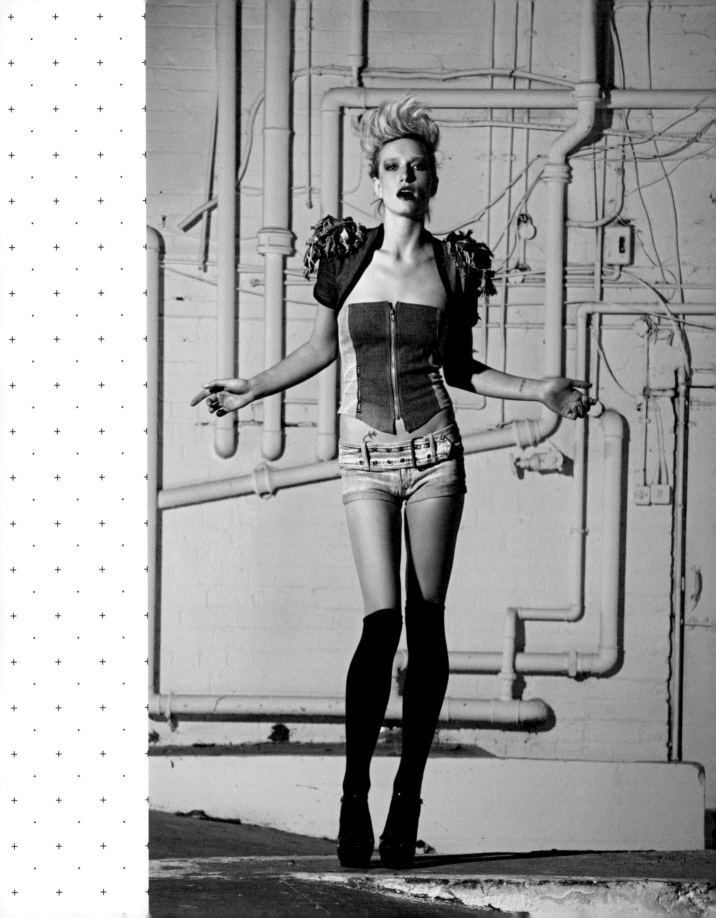

deconstructed by hand before being remodelled into entirely new creations directly on the mannequin, with little in common with their humble beginnings.

Han first started using recycled materials two years after graduating, when she entered a recycled-fashion competition in Liverpool. She discovered a real love for using recycled denim – the natural wear and fade (an ethical alternative to the harmful practice of sandblasting), as well as the textural quality, drew her to the material. Excited by the diversity of tone and weight, Han delights in mixing variously sourced denim in a single design to achieve both delicate and graphic effects. The diversion of damaged, second-hand jeans from landfill or deportation to developing countries, and a carbon-neutral output owing to her local sourcing and production process, validate her choice of raw material.

With a background in fashion design and freelance styling, Han has been making upcycled clothes for a number of years. She has an active role in Manchester's first sustainable fashion collective, 'Stitched Up', providing upcycling and sustainable fashion workshops to adults and children in the Manchester area, as well as educational information on alternatives to high-street consumerism. Han is writing her thesis for her Masters on, of course, sustainable fashion and upcycling. Passionate about ethical and sustainable development, she intends to continue playing a key role in the development of innovative and creative alternatives to fast fashion.

UTE
DECKER

A GERMAN-BORN ARTIST,
DESIGNER AND JEWELER,
UTE DECKER COMES FROM
A FAMILY OF ARTISAN
WINEMAKERS DATING BACK
TO THE SIXTEENTH CENTURY.

Decker grew up in the Rhine Valley, where she developed a deep respect for nature and craftsmanship. With a degree in political economics, Decker has travelled extensively, working in Paris and New York as a linguist, journalist and documentary film-maker. Her craft continues to inform her practice – she carefully considers her work in the contexts of society and the environment, while advocating sustainability.

Now based in London, Decker is an artist–maker who cares about every aspect of her craft and campaigns for ethical 'good practice' from mine to jewelry box. Her jewelry is made from fair-trade gold, 100 per cent recycled silver and bio resin derived from sunflowers to replace the more usual toxic option. Decker's fair-trade alluvial gold collection is extracted by artisanal miners without the use of chemicals, and reflects the purity of the gold's provenance through minimalist clean lines. Fifteen per cent of the fair-trade premium directly benefits small mining communities in Oro Verde, Colombia.

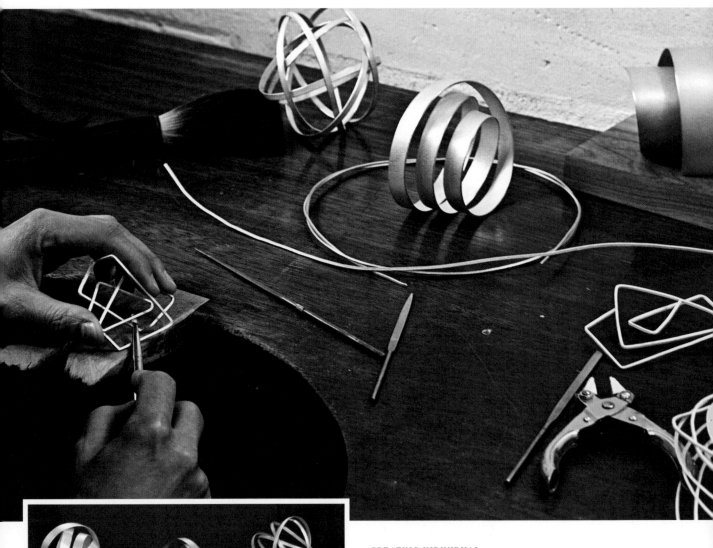

CREATING INDIVIDUAL
AND WEARABLE OBJETS
D'ART IN LIMITED EDITIONS,
NO TWO PIECES ARE
THE SAME IN SHAPE
OR TEXTURE OF FINISH.

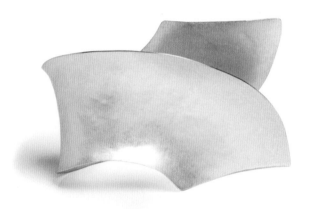

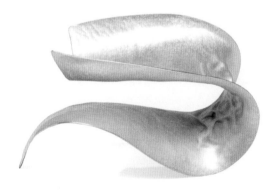

Decker's designs carry a meaning that transcends function. Her ethos is influenced by the ancient Japanese philosophy of wabi sabi and its fundamental concept of mindfulness, where the silence between notes in music and the harmony between form and space is vital, magnifying the intensity of expression. Leaving small marks from the work that went into each piece, Decker makes visible a humble recognition of our own flaws and imperfections. Her designs are Zen-like in their simplicity, akin to a Japanese master calligrapher's brushstroke, with sweeping lines never wavering in their serene beauty, but expressed through immense discipline. The clean formed lines of her wearable sculptures belie the complexity of process required to convey such surety and simplicity. With a penchant for curved lines, her designs gently coil around your wrist as if a gifted alchemist turned nature's own forms molten. Others have hard lines that mimic astronomical plots and planetary orbital projections, with interlocking arcs and curves.

For Decker, creating form is a very personal abstract expression of her ideas, values and aesthetic sensitivity. As a consequence, the beauty of her work is expressed not only in form, but also through material choice and provenance, the inherent qualities of the materials themselves, communicating beauty as virtue, alluding to trust, kindness, justice and courage. Through her work as a jeweler, Decker strives to acknowledge the complex relationship between beauty and ethics, outer and inner beauty. Process is key: Decker's designs develop their own character in the making, meaning that no one piece is the same. She is an artist who allows her work to gestate and naturally mature over time, culminating in, as she calls it, an 'architecture that can be inhabited', and not simply jewelry.

Steinwidder

DESIGNERS WORKING WITH UNUSED MATERIALS

An enormous amount of natural, chemical and human resources go into the production of new textiles and clothing, yet we discard an average of 15 per cent of them as a matter of course, 85 per cent of which is destined for landfill,[1] despite the fact that most textile products can be recycled or, at the very least, downcycled.

The mainstream fashion and apparel industry is an incredibly wasteful one, and like many conventional production industries, completely unsustainable over the long-term. Waste is created at every stage of production, from the growing, extraction or manufacturing of the fibre to the cleaning, spinning, dyeing, finishing, weaving, knitting, cutting and sewing of the garments. The results are damaged and leftover or unwanted fabric headers, proofs and sample weaves, knit and print tests and mistakes, lab dips, production cuttings, offcuts, overages and sewing errors. This is an enormous amount of waste and surplus that is traditionally considered an acceptable cost of production.

Textile production is the second largest industrial pollution source of clean water after agriculture.[2] An average pair of denim jeans, for example, takes up to 10,850 litres (3000 gallons) of water to produce.[3] This water use, known as the embedded water content, is the amount of water employed to grow and make things. There are approximately 450 million pairs of denim jeans sold annually in the USA, which amounts to nearly 5.2 trillion litres (1.4 trillion gallons) of water (equivalent to half of California's entire yearly urban water usage), just to produce denim jeans for the USA market alone!

At a time of water crises and shortage around the world and with over 780 million people denied access to fresh clean drinking water,[4] this is an unconscionable waste.

Sustainable design is about more than using ecological fibres; it is also about finding creative solutions for a system that is broken, and a means of making use of what others consider acceptable waste. It is the ability to see untapped resources where others see only damage and rubbish, and to find visionary solutions to unsustainable practices. There are a number of talented and creative designers revaluing and reimagining our industries' waste. Designers working with production offcuts and leftovers, seasonal headers from mills, dead stock fabric and the like have risen to the challenge of employing, in many cases, small pieces of fabric in limited and uncontrollable supply and in uncoordinated hues, textures and prints. In spite of the obvious drawbacks, however, there are also certain advantages of scale: headers are a standard dimension and offcuts are at production scale. It requires a discerning eye and an innate ability to mix and match colour and texture to work with leftover fabrics, as well as the ability to take advantage of unexpected treasures.

The use of upcycled textiles addresses the enormous waste in a system of production that is anything but sustainable, along with a system of waste generation that is never-ending. With all the inherent waste built into this system, it makes perfect sense to squeeze out every last drop of value from newly produced textiles. Finding sustainable and ecological means of doing business is no longer a choice; it is a requirement. Designers have the responsibility to learn from each other and to design more intelligently and more responsibly to ensure the sustainability and longevity of the fashion industry, as well as the planet. My part in that future is to honour and communicate the groundbreaking and cutting-edge work of those designers.

1 Published online at: earth911.com/recycling/household/ clothing-and-textile/facts-about-clothes/
2 Ibid.
3 Published online at: edro.wordpress.com/water/virtual- water-content/
4 Published online at: www.unicef.org/wash/index_3951.html

Hibrida

SAVE W
Save waste
Carmina Can
garbage bag
leather, they
creased as a
longer the c
we want to
the means
and

CARMINA
CAMPUS

THIS LABEL WORKS
EXCLUSIVELY WITH ALREADY
EXISTING MATERIALS, BOTH USED
AND UNUSED, RESCUED OUT
OF THE PRODUCTION AND
CONSUMPTION CYCLES TO MAKE
SUSTAINABLE PROJECTS, INCLUDING
BAGS, JEWELRY AND FURNITURE.

Ilaria Venturini Fendi, the youngest daughter of Anna Fendi, herself one of five sisters who transformed the Fendi family business into an international brand, founded Carmina Campus in 2006. Venturini uses the family brand's artisanal approach to refashion discarded and damaged materials into desirable objects made precious through premium craftsmanship. A project of creative sustainability, the label proposes small but effective solutions to environmental crises.

Bags are made from almost any material, and are often centred around a theme or issue. Collections are not seasonal; instead bags are grouped according to material. For example, shower curtains and other waterproof materials are used to draw attention to water issues, or rubbish bags of all kinds are employed to highlight the garbage crisis. Thinking way outside the box in terms of repurposing materials, other things used by Venturini include airplane seats, car seats, swatch books of all kinds, volleyball nets, old belts, Venetian blinds and cleaning sponges. If it is waste, Carmina Campus will find a creative use for it.

Amazing examples of innovative material use include the Switch bags, made from sample books of electrical plug cover plates (yes, electrical plugs, in everything from high-tech plastic to steel and wood), turned into decorative bag flaps on small clutch bags, with the body of the bag made from leather colour swatches or silk vintage fabrics, and the handle, a chain from a vintage belt or necklace. The Pyramid bags are formed from reclaimed offcuts of leather, cut into triangular shapes and stitched in a pyramid structure.

FROM WASTE.
als from being wasted.
orks with the big black
ubled and treated as
e stronger and thicker,
out skin. The bag is no
er to dispose whatever
of. Instead, it becomes
mbody sma
recover a n

FALLING ANGELS

The time-consuming manufacture is based on old shopping bags commonly used in Italy during wartime, when leather was difficult to find and bags were merely containers for shopping, not decorative accessories. The Swatch bags are produced from reclaimed colour swatch books from leather manufacturers, which are presented each season to showcase the in colours to buyers. Celebrating their reclamation, Venturini highlights their original use by using the code numbers and colour names. The swatches are attached to a base material of defective or end-of-line materials, such as mosquito netting, vintage lace, curtains, velvets, tie fabrics and scarves. Other versions of this line of bags are made from fur remnants and even from sample books of plastic or metal tiles from furniture and elevator producers.

Venturini has been working with African communities from the very beginning of the project and collaborates with the International Trade Centre, a joint United Nations and World Trade Organization agency, on the production of semi-finished parts to be employed in bags made in Italy, as well as a range made entirely by ITC communities in the slums of Korogocho, Nairobi. The bags are available in high-end fashion boutiques around the world, sending the message that sustainable can also be luxurious. Awarded the first Grand Prize by the World Fashion Development Programme (WFDP) by editor-in-chief of *Vogue Italia* and goodwill ambassador for Fashion4Development Franca Sozzani, Venturini was honoured as a distinguished innovator in the fashion industry, making efforts to make business more humane.

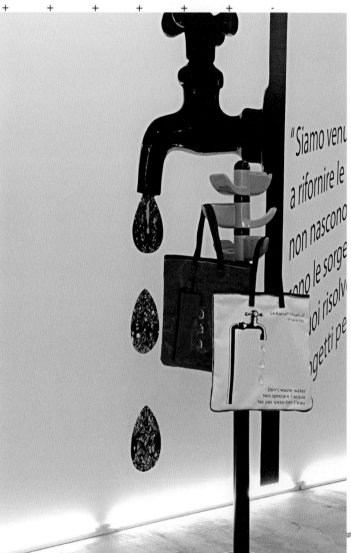

EVA ZINGONI

BY HER OWN ACCOUNT,
EVA ZINGONI IS ARGENTINEAN,
ITALIAN, SOMETIMES MADRILENIAN,
DEEPLY PARISIAN AND
COMPLETELY LATIN.

A traveller with boundless curiosity, eclectic taste and a cultivated independence, she is also the founder of her namesake label specializing in sustainable couture. Made entirely in France from recycled materials, Zingoni's designs are limited-edition pieces cut from surplus materials sourced from Parisian fashion houses. Unique fabrics, selected one by one, they constitute a collection based on recycled luxury.

With a resumé to boast about, Zingoni graduated from the Institut Français de la Mode, going on to translate trends for fashion soothsayer Li Edelkoort as well as Ralph Lauren. She then worked for six years at Balenciaga, where she was responsible for 'special requests', travelling the world and acting as the liaison between Nicolas Ghesquière and his red-carpet clients, such as Nicole Kidman, Salma Hayek and Charlotte Gainsbourg.

In 2008, Zingoni created her own collection, aiming to use her extensive couture experience to promote a different kind of fashion – an ethical fashion. Her sense of style is transcendent, not rooted in a season or a trend: a little bit of yesterday that is completely and utterly today. The philosophy behind the brand unites two opposites: her passion for fashion and her concept of activism. With no pretension of being an activist herself, she nevertheless holds dear the notion of making a difference through action, using her experience and her skill as the means for her type of eco-activism.

RECYCLED LUXURY FABRICS
ARE INDIVIDUALLY CHOSEN
FOR THE COLLECTION.

Despite her impressive career credentials, Zingoni remains rooted in her value system, unswayed by the antithetical values of the fashion system, believing that she must be true to her ideas as a means of achieving her own happiness, and happy to sacrifice her relative financial success and status en route. She comes from a background in political activism; her parents were both involved in the populist Peronist movement, known for its social justice and named after Juan Perón (married to Eva Perón).

Fabric sources come from Zingoni's experience in the couture industry, with materials direct from the fashion houses and their manufacturers. Leather, for example, comes from leftover couture production, where only the very perfect centres of skins are used and the rest – the greater part in many cases – is thrown away. She does not 'choose' the offcuts that the luxury industry rejects, but works instead with what she is given, making selections and connections between materials and what she would like to use in her collection. The difficulty always lies in making a whole of disparate pieces, and forming homogeneity with fabrics, textures and colours from different origins and time periods.

Fabrics are, nevertheless, the first inspiration in her work, just as they are for haute-couture designers, who are happy to work with some amazing and often very rare and very special materials. There ends the similarity to the haute-couture process, however, as Zingoni must make her designs fit not only the fabric qualities, but also the scale, limited as she is by the amount and size of offcuts. It is a way of working that she sees as growing out of the economic crisis, creating from what you have. Working to use and reuse existing patterns in a sustainable way, Zingoni must identify which fabrics suit which styles, making whatever subtle changes are needed to the pattern. In the end, this is a technical exercise to some degree, as different fabric combinations require different handling. Zingoni's collection is just as desirable as the designers' her offcuts are sourced from – in its way all the more luxurious for its use of limited, valued and scarce materials, and the skill and taste needed to employ them.

FRIENDS
WITH BENEFITS

DESCRIBING ITS COLLECTION AS
THE DEFINITION OF MODERN
DRESSING, AND HIGH FASHION
WITHOUT THE ATTITUDE, FRIENDS
WITH BENEFITS IS INSPIRED BY A
SENSE OF REFINED SIMPLICITY,
WHICH GIVES THE LINE A QUIET,
UNDERSTATED SOPHISTICATION.

Designs incorporate basic geometric shapes, including squares, triangles and circles, cleverly draped, wrapped and twisted to create refined asymmetric styles. With intelligent seaming, the silhouettes flow with the body for an effortlessly chic look. Produced in a range of monochromatic tones – cream, black and steely grey – designs are accented with unusual details. Exotic tapered leather insets at the shoulder and partially hidden jacket panels are paired with surprising textile combinations, such as handwoven wool herringbone and lace-printed cashmere, or python print with a modal jersey. Asymmetric hemlines, wraps, cowls and drapes undulate and cocoon to form a fluidly tailored collection with a hint of the unexpected.

Friends With Benefits comprises Clark Sabbat, a trained fashion designer with more than 20 years industry experience, and creative director Lynn Levoy. Before Friends With Benefits, Sabbat divided his time between designing for Paris and New York fashion houses. Partner and muse, Lynn Levoy has a degree in communications, a history of working in PR and a background in fashion styling with a celebrity client list. She is also an accomplished trend forecaster, who spends her time researching the market to ensure that Friends With Benefits stays ahead of the pack.

SOPHISTICATED AND
UNDERSTATED ASYMMETRIC
DRAPING, WITH A ROCK AND
ROLL EDGE, INFORMS THE
COLLECTION'S SIGNATURE.

Materials include bamboo and modal jersey as the base of the collection, with 'Limited Editions' of hand-dyed recycled T-shirt fabric re-cut into new designs. Draped from scratch, each item is unique or in a highly limited run, and produced in the USA. The collection is developed from two different perspectives: the innovative and the commercial. The 'Limited Editions' form the inspiration for the collection, serving as incubators for ideas, which are then realized with a business eye. Materials are sourced from vintage stores across the USA and abroad, as well as from flea markets and fabric manufacturers. With no special arrangements with manufacturers, Friends With Benefits relishes the challenges that limitation enforces: each item is an individual piece of wearable art. Working directly on the mannequin, the designers cut and pin directly, feeling their way as they go, letting the silhouette develop without over-thinking the process, and allowing their experience combined with a sense of daring to lead the way.

Sabbat is influenced by the fashion greats, such as Madame Grès and Vionnet and their sense of architecture, where each line has a meaning. Sabbat strives for simplicity in everything he designs, adhering to the concept that simplicity is the most difficult thing to achieve. Music plays a major role in the creation of the collection, and is a constant accompaniment to their work, coming from their extensive music library of over 30,000 songs. With a huge collection of imagery from a multitude of vintage and current sources, Friends With Benefits reinterprets every visual inspiration from old movies to the street through their own aesthetic. Sabbat nevertheless cites his wife and business partner as his main influence and only muse – her personal sense of style and natural elegance leads the creative process both directly and indirectly.

THE COLLECTION IS FASHIONED FROM
HAND-DYED RECYCLED T-SHIRT
FABRIC, WITH EACH UNIQUE PIECE
BEING DRAPED FROM SCRATCH.

FROM SOMEWHERE

THIS BRITISH LABEL WAS BORN OF A LOVE OF VINTAGE, PROVINCIAL HABERDASHERIES, BEAUTIFUL CLOTHES AND EXQUISITE ARTISANSHIP.

DESIGNERS WORKING WITH UNUSED MATERIALS

The founder, Orsola de Castro, has been trying to find the next logical step to recycling the fashion industry's pre-consumer waste for some time. Her label, on London's Portobello Road, has long since reflected her heritage as well as her and her partner Filippo Ricci's ethos. Working with some of the finest manufacturers in Italy, De Castro has managed to forge long-term partnerships through recycling the fashion industry's premium waste – reimagining and refashioning cutting-room scraps, end of rolls, damaged goods and manufacturers' headers into fun, playful and well-designed dresses and separates.

Founded in 1997, From Somewhere began with a small capsule collection of second-hand sweaters and cardigans, rescued from landfill and individually customized with elaborate crochet detailing. It was during a trip to a factory in Italy that De Castro realized that the discarded scraps of fabric on the floor were potentially a valuable resource if viewed from a different perspective. All of From Somewhere's collections are now made with luxury designer pre-consumer waste. Each piece is individually cut, with an eclectic and original use of colour and paneling, making From Somewhere pieces instantly recognizable. The beauty of each piece is in its uncompromising balance between contemporary design and a poetic and ethical solution to waste.

Enter Speedo: with thousands of unusable and unsaleable LZR racer suits and fabric after the Fédération Internationale de Natation's (FINA) ruling that full body suits would be banned from competitive swimming, Speedo was left with sizeable stock and no end users. And, if you were not a competitive

THE SPEEDO DESIGN
COLLABORATION HAS
EXTENDED ACROSS MULTIPLE
SEASONS, THANKS TO FROM
SOMEWHERE'S PLAYFUL
APPROACH TO FASHION
AND CREATIVE REINVENTION
OF SOURCE MATERIALS.

DESIGNERS WORKING WITH UNUSED MATERIALS

swimmer looking to shave split seconds off your time, why would you want a swimsuit that extends from neck to wrist to ankle? As it turned out, Orsola de Castro wanted them. Here was the opportunity she had been looking for: wasted materials in production scale to recycle and redesign. In an unusual display of vision for a global multinational brand – usually more concerned about maintaining the integrity of its logo than the ecological implications of incinerating thousands of suits – Speedo decided to explore new ways of using their excess stock, offering the suits to artistic and creative groups. And so the limited-edition capsule collection by From Somewhere in collaboration with Speedo was born.

With complicated cutting and slashing, each step christened with ironic names like 'leg to gusset cut', 'horizontal boob cut' and 'straight over gusset cut', De Castro turned the suits into an edgy fashion collection, replete with frills, stripes and brilliant colour insertions. The first Speedo capsule collection consisted of ten styles, including a statement dress, a range of floor-grazing evening wear, short and sassy retro dresses, quirky body-conscious separates and high-fashion pieces. The collection was launched exclusively in Selfridges in the UK during Climate Week; it was then released by yoox.com to coincide with International Earth Day.

De Castro and Ricci have managed to build unique relationships with manufacturers and suppliers, gaining their trust by showing the integrity of their designs and their business practices. Breaking ground in the world of recycled fashion, From Somewhere continues to work with major manufacturers and producers, and is now in its third season of the Speedo collaboration.

GOODONE

A CONTEMPORARY, INDEPENDENT, LONDON-BASED FASHION LABEL, GOODONE USES RECLAIMED FABRICS TO CREATE A DESIRABLE COLLECTION THAT REFLECTS ITS ENVIRONMENT.

With a quirky, London aesthetic that runs the gamut of London looks, from sophisticated and original to feminine and playful, the brand never takes itself too seriously. Somewhere between the style of the clothes in the film *The Fifth Element* and a vintage mix-and-match approach, Goodone toys with unusual and imbalanced colour combinations. The designers work with offcuts and excess fabric from the fashion industry. Renowned for their pieced and panelled, body-conscious dresses and jumpers, the label also incorporates accessories such as mittens, muffs and chunky cable-knit belts.

Fully integrated in the mainstream fashion industry, Goodone is committed to positive change from within. The company sources its fabrics from both pre- and post-consumer waste, hand-picking unwanted garments from recycling factories and gathering scraps, sample fabric yardage and ends of rolls from textile mills and factories. The designers then mix it all up with new British-made and dyed sustainable fabrications, wherever possible. Good design is priority number one for Goodone, even when making conscientious choices. Proving that sustainability and good design are not mutually exclusive, the collection

KNOWN FOR BOLD COLOUR-
BLOCKED STYLING, GOODONE'S
DESIGN METHOD IS INFORMED
BUT NOT RESTRAINED BY THE
USE OF RECYCLED FABRICS.

has an easy-wear aesthetic, with a touch of boho and designer chic mixed in. With a sophisticated eye for colour and texture, Goodone makes some unexpected combinations with a certain French flair for elegance and a polished competence. It achieves the kind of casual sense of style so often seen on Parisians, who naturally mix ethnic with designer and vintage looks for an eclectic but pulled-together look. The collection is body conscious and simultaneously oversized, in knits, silk and suede.

Goodone's collaborations read like a list of Who's Who. With NOKI, the label produced pieces shown at London Fashion Week as part of Fashion East. Goodone has also worked with Amnesty International, Liberty of London, the World Wildlife Fund, Greenpeace, Shelter and No Sweat. The company was part of a project that upcycled campaign T-shirts, and also created a limited-edition dress for the Fashion Targets Breast Cancer campaign, launching a manufacturing partnership with HEBA Women's Project. Goodone has produced a limited-edition bag in collaboration with Puma, offers a collection available at Topshop and designs recycled pieces for Tesco. Goodone founder Nin Castle is the recipient of many awards, including the Trefor Campbell Award for Creative Enterprise and the Small Medium Enterprise (SME) Innovation Award. It has received sponsorships and mentorships from the British Fashion Council and the Greater London Enterprise to exhibit at Pure, UK. The collection is shipped worldwide and sold online from its own e-commerce site as well as through ASOS. Goodone's collection is shown at London Fashion Week.

Using reclaimed fabrics in every possible part of the process, Goodone creates desirable feminine pieces to wear from day to evening. The label gives women the opportunity to feel good about their clothes and to work with what already exists to achieve more.

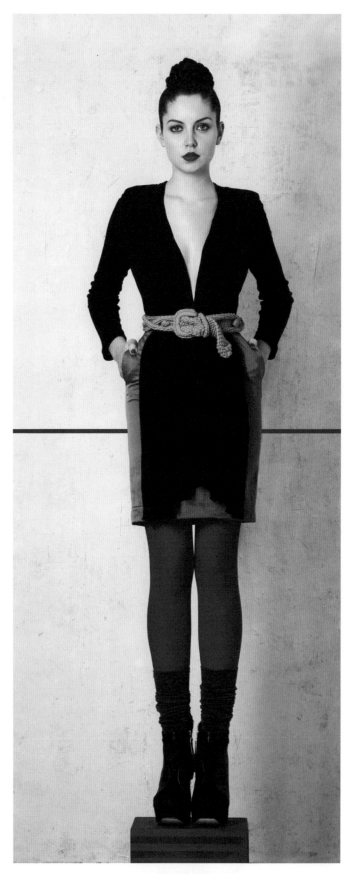

HIBRIDA

ART-HOUSE ACCESSORIES LABEL HIBRIDA TRANSFORMS RECOVERED AND DISCARDED MATERIALS THROUGH DESIGN AND CRAFTSMANSHIP TO PRODUCE A CONTEMPORARY AVANT-GARDE COLLECTION OF BODY ORNAMENTATION.

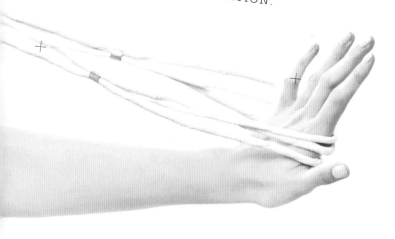

Motivated to create beautiful objects, full of symbolic meaning, Hibrida infuses materials with new value, prolonging their life and diverting them from landfill. The concept behind the collection is a hybrid design process – hence the name – inspired by an abstraction of elements, new and old, contemporary and vintage, valued and discarded. Establishing a past and a present through its mixed textile use, carrying identity and characteristics from the past and fusing them with updated material, the brand affirms its connection with the present.

The project strives to create and manage independence. Partners Angélica Delgado, a theatre designer, and Eduardo Sepúlveda, an interdisciplinary and experimental artist, jointly explore the fields of recycling, textiles and fashion jewelry. They seek to establish a clear identity that integrates different aspects of ecology through clothing, jewelry, textiles and accessories. The collection explores spatial composition through architectural form and dimension to create alien forms worthy of a princess from another planet on a designer *Star Trek*.

The label's conceptual designs mix fabrics to create a visual language that reuses waste experimentally. Cognizant of the deeper cultural significance of textiles, Hibrida consciously crosses and overlaps fabrics from different times, bringing the iconographic, technical, aesthetic and cultural connection of the materials to the forefront. Exploring ways to rework biomorphic three-dimensional volume through timeless imagery and to create using existing resources, Hibrida seeks to draw attention to our values and the workmanship in creation, design and handwork (rather than through material choice). Aware of the large volume of raw material discarded daily, and the associated environmental problems, the company devised a means to reuse and reduce waste through experimentation, aiming to convey a message of awareness. Mimicking nature's own no-waste philosophy, where nothing is destroyed, merely transformed, Hibrida opens a dialogue about the relationship between people and their environment.

Established in 2008 after observing the enormous amount of textile waste generated by small-scale producers in the sector, Hibrida proposed a pilot project that employed the factories' waste as the raw material for creation. Materials are collected through strategic alliances with fashion designers, and intended to reduce surplus production by using factory overages, offcuts, excess trimmings, cuttings, fragments, damaged goods and selvedges. Material is separated and categorized by type, size and colour. Hibrida also works with vintage textile bales and garments, including upholstery fabric, burlap and sacks, and the thread recovered from disposable PET bottles. Inspiration for the creative stage is informed by pre-Columbian cultures and traditional craftsmanship, and draws on Latin America's rich heritage of techniques.

Hibrida's 'Bio-Morph' collection uses the technique of barrel stitching to produce organic forms that reflect nature, where nothing is created or destroyed, only transformed. The pieces are presented in three stages: closed circular contoured shapes with clearly concentric tubular forms, giving way to folds and curls and culminating in random structures. Each piece is sewn entirely by hand and finished with silver to produce three-dimensional volumetric and wearable pieces of art. Designs are futuristic and conceptual, with a vintage B-movie twist, worthy of any visiting dignitary from another universe.

THE INTERDISCIPLINARY
ART-HOUSE ACCESSORIES
LABEL DIVERTS UNWANTED
AND USED TEXTILES FROM
LANDFILL TO CREATE ITS
ABSTRACT ARTWEAR.

JUANA DÍAZ

SANTIAGO-BASED JUANA DÍAZ (JD)
IS BOTH A FASHION DESIGNER
AND A TEXTILE ARTIST, WORKING
WITH FABRIC SCRAPS TO GENERAT
EXCLUSIVE HANDCRAFTED
PRODUCTS THROUGH FAIR LABOUR
WITH FEMALE HOMEWORKERS.

Developing a technique that cobbles together varying scraps of fabric, using her signature contrasting topstitching to bridge the textural, colour and scale diversity between fabrics, JD produces simple kimono-style tops and wrap dresses, which belie the complicated nature of the fabric piecing and stitch overlays. Layering and asymmetric cuts add further complexity to the volume and silhouette. Her stitching and patching techniques evoke comparison to the creation of mosaics, or stained-glass windows, with their strong visual texture and colour combinations. Mostly produced from a mix of menswear suits, with a rich mélange of twills, herringbones and pinstripes, raw and frayed edges, all pieces incorporate a single monochromatic cross-stitched topstitching. JD also works with brilliant dashes of colour in the form of scarlet and gold, punctuating the otherwise subtle blend of her coordinating materials. Understated coats and jackets have brightly patchworked backs, while skirts and tops rely on contrasting tabs and ties for fastening, often with embroidered sayings adorning the hems and underskirts.

Working in opposition to the mainstream fashion industry, where waste is built into the system through production, labour abuse and the seasonal presentation of a collection, Díaz creates a collection built around waste and textile scraps. Her ethical fashion project 'Fabric of the Future' integrates into the fashion system vulnerable workers in the manufacturing process. The project seeks to decrease the damage caused to the environment through the fashion industry by recovering textile scraps discarded from traditional garment manufacture, creating new fabrics and giving life to new garments. Women homemakers, who require a flexible work schedule in order to tend to their children, produce the collection. Díaz also works and trains socially vulnerable people from marginalized communities, such as prison inmates and recently released prisoners who face difficulties entering the world of work. By using materials at no or low cost, Díaz is able to pay her employees a fair wage while training them, helping her to achieve a standard of work well above the industry norm.

Díaz's work has been described as futuristic and beautiful, conveying the feeling of a strange and disturbing future. Fragmented and scarred fabrics, found after a disaster, compose the collection's base. Languid models pace distractedly on the catwalk, as if preoccupied by some imminent and inevitable catastrophe. Díaz often uses the catwalk, as well as the clothes themselves, to conceal or reveal social messages. Sometimes described as a fashion terrorist, JD has also created costumes for the Ballet Nacional de Chile, film and theatre, and has taught workshops at various educational institutions.

Winning accolades and awards across Latin America for her collection, Díaz is a fashion activist, using her medium to portray her beliefs and to act as a catalyst to achieve change within the industry. An outspoken critic of public and governmental policy, Díaz has used her platform to speak out about Chilean law on salmon fishing and the leasing of fishing areas along the coast. Using the catwalk to protest against the laws passed, the models hold signs saying, 'The Fisheries Act for Fishermen' and 'free the sea'. Benefits from the show were donated to a fund for fishermen who had lost their boats during the earthquake and tsunami in 2010.

DÍAZ'S SIGNATURE CONTRASTING TOPSTITCH JOINS TOGETHER TEXTILE SCRAPS DISCARDED FROM TRADITIONAL GARMENT MANUFACTURE.

SOMETIMES DESCRIBED
AS A FASHION TERRORIST,
DÍAZ UTILIZES THE CATWALK
TO COMMUNICATE SOCIAL
AND POLITICAL PERSPECTIVES.

CONTEMPORARY JEWELER AND
ARTIST KERRY HOWLEY EXPLORES
THE POWER THAT MATERIALS
HAVE TO ELICIT AN EMOTIONAL
RESPONSE TO JEWELRY.

KERRY HOWLEY

CAMBRIDGE-BASED DESIGNER KERRY HOWLEY PRODUCES AN EXQUISITELY FINE, FILIGREED COLLECTION OF NECKLACES MADE FROM A VERY UNUSUAL MATERIAL: DISCARDED HUMAN HAIR.

The collection is entitled 'Attraction/Aversion' and comprises five necklaces sculpted entirely from hair. Howley focuses on our visceral and cultural connection to materials, investigating how some materials provoke conflicting emotional responses. Through her material choice, Howley incites feelings of attraction and aversion. Hair has a unique place in Western culture, evoking pride and familiarity when clean, healthy and still attached, yet triggering feelings of disgust and repulsion when detached, and blocking a drain, for example. Working with delicate and intricate patterns, Howley seeks to combine these two opposing emotions into a pleasing whole. Carefully deconstructing the cultural codes of hair and pattern in our society, she juxtaposes instinctual responses. Pleasing pattern and form and delicate and intricate adornment are composed from a material that results from us, thereby exploring ideas of emotional conflict through design.

Building on an ancient history of the incorporation of human hair in jewelry, as in memento mori, Howley finds an entirely new means by which to wear lost hair again, adding a layer of irony, verging on perversion, to her intellectually and emotionally challenging work. The theoretically contrasting emotional responses of attraction and aversion are sometimes oddly congruous, with repulsion often laced with fascination and intrigue. The necklaces are an outgrowth of her second-year degree research on circuses and freak shows in Victorian England, leading to her interest in the grotesque through exploration of conflicting responses.

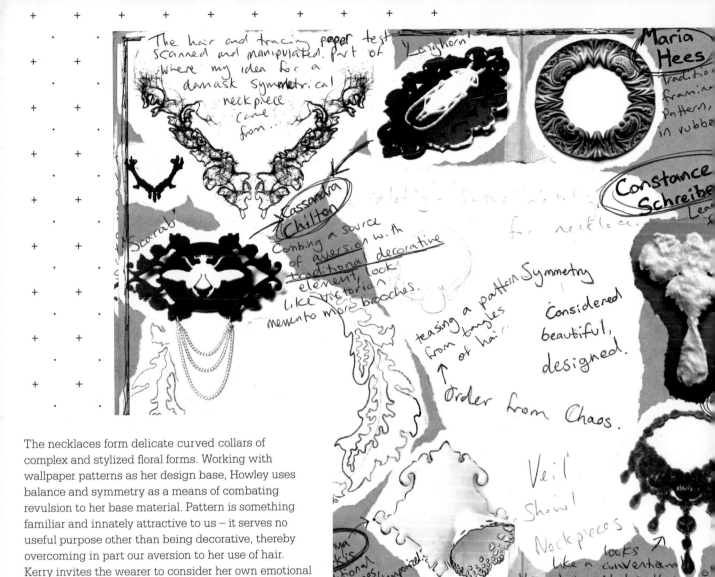

The necklaces form delicate curved collars of complex and stylized floral forms. Working with wallpaper patterns as her design base, Howley uses balance and symmetry as a means of combating revulsion to her base material. Pattern is something familiar and innately attractive to us – it serves no useful purpose other than being decorative, thereby overcoming in part our aversion to her use of hair. Kerry invites the wearer to consider her own emotional responses, and the delicate balance between attraction and aversion.

Each of the five necklaces took more than sixty hours to create. Working with donated hair from a friend's mother, Howley began by rolling it in her hands to make it matted and tangled and, therefore, easier to work with. The fineness and delicacy of the work, combined with the difficulty of the material, meant that she had to work directly on top of her drawn design, using a needle to hold down the hair in the required place. Fingers were simply too large and clumsy for work of this detail, so the fine teeth of a jeweler's saw blade encouraged the hair in a particular direction. The hair was then fixed with fast-setting resin glue.

Howley's graduate collection for Middlesex University received the Arthur Silver Award for Graduate Innovation and Excellence in 2011. Her work has been showcased in museum exhibitions exploring our response to the body, such as 'ULTRABODY' at the Castello Sforzesco in Milan. Howley also undertakes special 'hair' commissions through her own website, often not as jewelry, but instead intended for display. Howley is exploring more wearable versions of her work produced from raw silk fibres in place of human hair.

THE EXPLORATION OF RIBBON
ART AND ORIGAMI-LIKE FOLDING
TECHNIQUES FORMS THE BASIS
OF THE COLLECTION, IN
COMBINATION WITH THRIFT-
SHOP FINDS, DISCARDED
ACCESSORIES AND FLOCKING.

MICHELLE LOWE-HOLDER

INSPIRED TO CREATE TREASURE FROM TRASH, MICHELLE LOWE-HOLDER BUILDS ON HER LOVE OF TRADITIONAL TEXTILES THROUGH AN ONGOING EXPERIMENTATION WITH TRADITIONAL AND HISTORIC TECHNIQUES WITH A STRONG CRAFT HERITAGE.

Launched in London landmark fashion store Browns, and awarded the British Fashion Council's NEWGEN Award at London Fashion Week in 2001, Michelle Lowe-Holder was known primarily for her eponymous, feminine and wearable collections. Centred around ethical and sustainable concepts in one form or another, Lowe-Holder took a major new direction with her Autumn/Winter 10/11 collection and the launch of a completely sustainable accessories line entitled 'Ribbon Reclaim'. It is produced in its entirety from reclaimed and vintage ribbons, trims and recovered hardware. Hand-picked by the Centre for Sustainable Fashion, part of the London College of Fashion, the collection was presented at Somerset House as part of London Fashion Week.

Each season builds on the previous one, expanding and exploring new directions in a logical progression of material use and methods. Paying homage to the skill of embroiderers from the Middle Ages, Lowe-Holder combines the use of end-of-line textiles and handcrafted ribbon art with industrially flocked, chunky hardware closures. All pieces in the line are ethically produced and sampled in the UK, for example, ribbons are laser cut and embellished with hand crochet. The collection is a great example of upcycling waste to create desirable pieces that have been transformed through her unique, feminine and modern style. The items are whimsical and flirtatious, with a strong historical connection, reminiscent of Elizabethan ruffs, some so light they almost look as if they might be capable of flight if it were not for the

UPCYCLING THROUGH
HER USE OF END-OF-LINE
MATERIALS, LOWE-HOLDER
ADHERES TO SUSTAINABLE
AND ETHICAL PRACTICES
OF ZERO WASTE.

repurposed heavy industrial metal closures. An avid collector of vintage ribbons from the old warehouses in the area surrounding her studio in London's East End, Lowe-Holder also hoards vintage finds from markets as far afield as Canada and offcuts from previous collections. Working directly with her stashed and stored materials, Lowe-Holder sometimes creates up to 100 swatches for a single collection. Also working with leather offcuts and Kefi, a sustainably produced paperlike fabric from Italy, Lowe-Holder intricately weaves her vintage floral ribbons in and out of shiny metal links, adding a very modern interpretation to the ancient art of ribbon craft. Intricate origami folds of the crocodile- and snakeskin-embossed Kefi result in oversized neck and wrist cuffs, tying in with Lowe-Holder's inspiration from Victorian flowers and albino crocodiles.

Extending her vision of individuality and character into each season's lookbook, Lowe-Holder carefully selects her models, not from the world of fashion modelling, but instead from the street, and for the character and style they embody. As a means of exploring and exposing a wide range of beauty, the models exemplify curvaceous, Rubenesque forms, gracefully aging dancers, bald, pierced and pink-haired models, ghostly pale and dark skinned, each one embodying beauty in a real, diverse sense of the word. Photographer Polly Penrose and Lowe-Holder have made a conscious effort not to be constrained by the dictates of the fashion industry. While expanding their visual vocabulary, they are intent on finding an uneasy balance between confrontation, rawness and beauty, creating a range of portraits that showcase Lowe-Holder's provocative jewelry collection.

PLIZGA SOURCES HER
BROAD RANGE OF MATERIALS
FROM FLEA MARKETS,
SECOND-HAND GARMENTS
AND FACTORY OFFCUTS.

PAULINA PLIZGA

INSPIRED BY THE VOLUME
AND FORM OF POLISH SCULPTORS
MAGDALENA ABAKANOWICZ
AND WLADYSLAW HASIOR,
PARISIAN DESIGNER
PAULINA PLIZGA CREATES
ARTISTIC AND WEARABLE
TEXTILE COMPOSITIONS,
NO LESS POETIC IN TERMS
OF COMPOSITION,
VOLUME AND TEXTURE.

The depth and multitude of delicate textural tone-on-tone combinations deftly complement and contrast with each other to form a single design. The unfinished edges and rough serged seams belie the delicacy of the work, which suggests a boudoir sensibility, embodying a purity in its naïvety and rejoicing in the imperfection of detail, and each run and hole. Every design is unique. There is some repetition in style, but totally different fabric combinations make no two pieces the same.

Plizga's designs are realized in a broad range of materials that include scraps of couture fabrics and discarded plastic and paper. Sourcing some of her best snippets from flea markets and second-hand garments, Plizga also uses factory offcuts and donations, and end-of-line couture fabrics purchased from the small stores of Montmartre.

With a particular love of wool and brocade, laces and all kinds of transparent materials (including organza, silk and muslin), Plizga first sorts her fabric finds by colour. Then each piece is shredded into small strips and pinned on to a simple underlay, from which Plizga constructs a new fabric from scratch, by over-stitching the strips of material together. She creates unique crazy patchworks inspired by nature and incorporating tangled threads and post-consumer recycled waste, constructing them like a bird's nest. Working directly on the mannequin, Plizga never uses paper patterns, but interweaves her shreds of sheer fabrics, brocades and lace with knits, which naturally conform to the body's contours.

Designer and artist, Polish-born Plizga showed her first collection in Paris at the famous Place des Vosges in 1994. After years of observing the French couture masters, museum research and independent practice at the side of her dressmaker mother, she learned her fascination for fabric leftovers, all leading to her Paris debut. From that day on, Plizga has steadily built a client base of faithful customers, first selling at alternative fashion fairs, then boutiques and now in stores internationally from Tokyo to Paris and London to Strasbourg.

Known for her open-studio environments, she loves to work directly, transparently and publicly with her customers. She spent two weeks working in a reconstructed studio, under the name Trash Factory, in the public space of Tokyo's Laforet shopping centre; the experience led her to strengthen, grow and liberate her artistic expression and creative process into open studio events. She brings the creative process to the forefront, which has allowed her to detach from the traditional fashion show format. Expanding on the Trash Factory concept, Plizga has performed similar open-studio concepts in Berlin, Edinburgh and Vienna. Each time she expands the breadth of her expression to incorporate fashion with video projection and live painting.

Expanding further on her creative expression, Plizga has been working on a collection entitled 'Nest' since 2008. Inspired by the old Japanese legend of *Tsuru no Ongaeshi* or Woman Crane, in which a simple farmer's kindness toward a wounded crane is repaid, the mixed-art installation incorporates hanging clothes, paintings and video projections, and has been presented in both Paris and the Czech Republic.

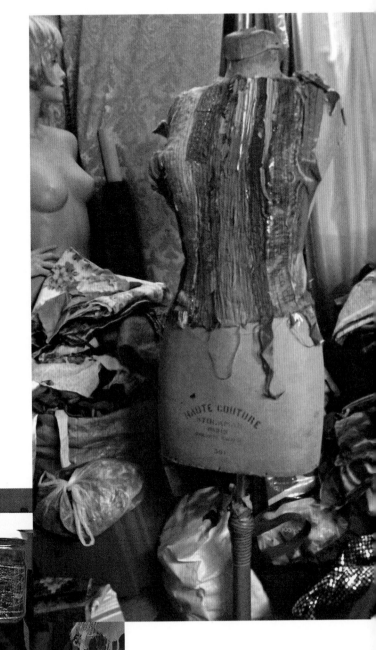

PIECING TOGETHER TINY SCRAPS OF DISCARDED TEXTILES THROUGH PATCHWORK, PLIZGA OFTEN CELEBRATES THE GARMENT'S CONSTRUCTION AS A FEATURE.

DESIGNERS WORKING WITH UNUSED MATERIALS

PIECE X PIECE

A WOMEN'S CONTEMPORARY
HIGH-FASHION COLLECTION,
PIECE X PIECE REVEALS A STORY
OF DISCARDED LUXURY.

Limited-edition pieces are inspired by San Francisco's urban landscape and produced from an ever-changing stock of luxury textile-industry discards. This is a personal response to the overwhelming amount of waste produced by the fashion industry. Textile and garment manufacture as a matter of course throws away thousands of fabric swatches each season, along with damages and factory offcuts, and the leftovers from garment production. They take the traditional route from fabric mill and garment manufacturer direct to landfill. Piece x Piece imagines new lives for these unwanted scraps, piecing them together to form a new whole, hence the name, and making wearable, contemporary clothing.

With a background in interior architecture, Elizabeth Brunner founded the sustainable label in 2008, based on the concept that existing materials are a precious resource with untapped potential. The result of reclamation, experimentation and design, each garment is unique. Her mission is to create beauty from waste, while working toward a new understanding of what waste really means, through revaluation, reuse and redesign. Collaborating with major design firms and high-street giants in the UK, Brunner went back to school to study fashion design at California College of the Arts. Combining all her training with a passion for sustainability, she meaningfully addresses material waste in the fashion industry.

Garments are produced in limited editions, are season-less in nature and timeless in design. The collection has a youthful innocence, at once easy to wear and easy on the eye, always flirtatious, and with the occasional touch of the tomboy. All patchwork and piecing is done with a very careful attention to colour, shape and texture. The manufacturing and sourcing process is extremely involved and time consuming, with each scrap of fabric carefully chosen and coordinated with others, and then pieced and placed to form a garment. Picking through designer waste to ensure that everything can be used, Brunner sources most fabrics within the USA, in particular from New York and Los Angeles.

With fabric, scale, colour, print and weave all varying from season to season, it is not always possible to create appealing garments. Therefore, Piece x Piece works on a small collection of home goods to better use certain colours and textures that lend themselves more readily to interior rather than fashion design. Any unusable scraps are donated to a local pattern-making school, conveniently located in the same building as the studio.

Some designs are produced from a combination of recycled and new materials, but all new fabrics are either sustainable or eco-friendly, such as bamboo and hemp. All recycled materials are pre-consumer waste, meaning that they are sourced directly from designers, who donate their leftover sample remnants and production offcuts (Piece x Piece sometimes works with scraps as small as 20 x 25 cm [8 x 10 inches]). The label has long-running relationships with six designers who regularly donate their end-of-season waste. Piece x Piece promotes this collaboration through features and links on its website.

RACHEL FREIRE

An artist at heart, she trained in fine arts, only to recognize that she did not want her work only to be admired in the rarified atmosphere of an art gallery. She then undertook theatre studies, but ended up in fashion after the realization that she wanted her artistic expression to be lived in. A self-described 'artist in wolf's clothing', she references the cut-throat industry in which she now works. Aiming to create previously non-existent worlds through design, Freire relishes the juxtaposition of opposites, making sense of the nonsensical, fusing them in such a way that their logic cannot be denied despite their obvious differences. 'Clothing is our means of self-expression, and should amplify our sense of self and uniqueness', she explains. Freire toys with masculine and feminine, bored of androgyny; she prefers to intensify one or the other, or both at the same time. Drawing inspiration from the past, she revels in militaristic classic lines, combined with daring dreams of a new future. As she says, 'Most of our lives these days are spent in a fantasy world, hiding from one reality or another, so why not dress for the party?'

Freire is best known for a range of beautifully designed pieces constructed from delicate powder-pink and deep matt black leather rosettes, juxtaposed with harsh militaristic pouches and straps and dominatrix-like corsetry spines. Designs simultaneously cover and reveal, all the while disguising their source material.

FUTURISTIC, ROMANTIC AND
DELICATE PIECES CONSTRUCTED
ENTIRELY FROM DISCARDED COW
NIPPLES ARE A VISUAL, CREATIVE
AND CEREBRAL INVESTIGATION
INTO BEAUTY AND RESPONSE.

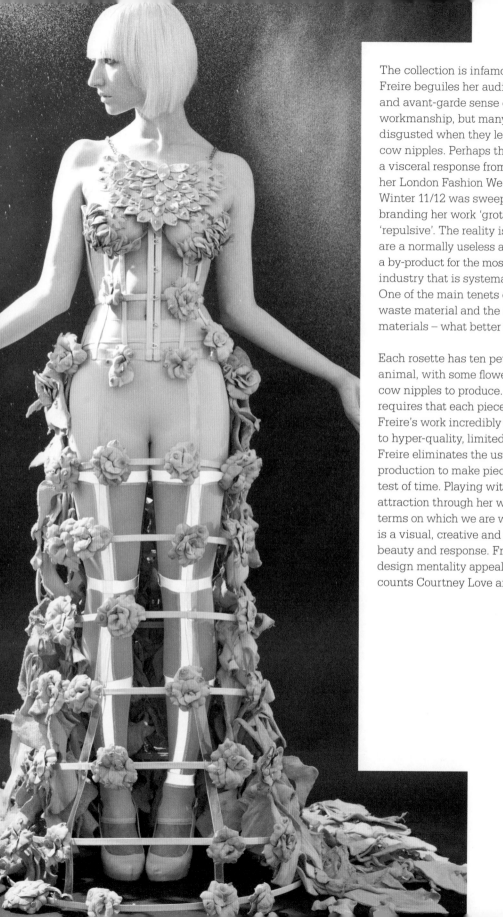

The collection is infamous because of the material use; Freire beguiles her audience with her sophisticated and avant-garde sense of design and exquisite workmanship, but many admirers are horrified and disgusted when they learn of her source material: cow nipples. Perhaps the nature of her material elicited a visceral response from the viewer, as the press from her London Fashion Week presentation for Autumn/ Winter 11/12 was sweeping, judgemental and brutal, branding her work 'grotesque', 'sickening' and 'repulsive'. The reality is, however, that cow nipples are a normally useless and wasted part of the cowhide, a by-product for the most part from the meat-processing industry that is systematically discarded as valueless. One of the main tenets of eco-design is the use of waste material and the revaluation of underappreciated materials – what better example could you find?

Each rosette has ten petals, each from a different animal, with some flowers taking as many as 3000 cow nipples to produce. The dimension of the material requires that each piece is handcrafted, making Freire's work incredibly labour intensive. Committed to hyper-quality, limited-edition, small-run productions, Freire eliminates the usual waste from seasonal production to make pieces of quality that stand the test of time. Playing with the themes of disgust and attraction through her work, Freire challenges the terms on which we are willing to see things. Her work is a visual, creative and cerebral investigation into beauty and response. Freire's controversial, intelligent design mentality appeals to other artists, and she counts Courtney Love and Beth Ditto as clients.

R.DS (RECYCLING DEAD STOCK)

A CONTEMPORARY DANISH UNISEX BRAND, R.DS IS INSPIRED BY VINTAGE MATERIALS AND TAILORED WITH NEW AND INNOVATIVE CUTS AND LINES.

Representing simple functional design with a twist, the label creates an individual look through its focus on fabric. Made entirely in Italy, the collection uses 100 per cent wool and cotton dead stock fabrics from some of the very best catwalk brands in Europe. With a passion for quality fabrication, the brand focuses on easy-going clothing and timeless genderless styles. The utilitarian and urban militaristic look is sensitively balanced by subtle colour and textural combinations. Recycling dead stock is at the core of R.ds's approach to fashion, and leads to the exclusivity of the designs, as garments cannot be mass-produced. Each piece acquires an inimitable quality through the piecing together of limited fabric resources, and in so doing battles unnecessary waste and promotes sustainable production methods.

The company was founded after Stine Christa Busk fell in love with the textile heritage of Prato, an area just outside Florence, famous for its textile tradition. The beauty and quality of the fabrics produced in the area was such that Stine and her partner Henrik Busk felt compelled to use every last scrap, leaving nothing to go to waste. Their first forays into reusing the fabrics began with the patchwork scarf, made from small squares of carefully matched and patched complementary wool textiles and framed by a luxurious mitre-cornered binding. This led to the pieced and patched military-style trousers.

INSPIRED BY VINTAGE TAILORING, R.DS APPROACHES THE CREATION OF ITS FASHION WITH A DISTINCTIVE STYLE AND EXCLUSIVITY.

The factories and producers that Stine and Henrik work with routinely produce for the likes of Armani, Prada and Jil Sander, so these are no ordinary factory offcuts, rather luxury leftovers. With a preference for natural and subtle colour combinations, something the chosen factories and brands specialize in, R.ds carefully constructs its sustainable designs. Sourcing and production is all done locally in Italy, with the materials all going to a small Italian workshop close by, where selection and production take place. The colour and pattern combination for the patchwork is entirely entrusted to the talented seamstresses on site, with whom the label has a relationship based on respect. R.ds is still in its formative stages, but the process of reusing these quality fabrics has felt right from the start.

Launched in the autumn of 2011, R.ds comes from a strong heritage of Danish high-end production through sister label Royal Buddha, which specializes in combining classic design with fine craftsmanship. Working from original USA military jackets, Royal Buddha richly embellishes each one with artisanal embroideries of Buddha. Also founded by Busk, the label produces high-quality underwear for The Royal Danish Ballet. The two brands play off and benefit from each other; Far Eastern and European trips searching for production for one often lead to sourcing opportunities for the other.

THE PIECED AND PATCHWORKED SCARF COMPRISES 10 DIFFERENT WOOL AND CASHMERE SWATCHES LEFT OVER FROM INTERNATIONAL FASHION HOUSES.

REET AUS

ESTONIAN FASHION AND
COSTUME DESIGNER DR REET AUS
RESEARCHES A MEANS TO
RADICALLY REDESIGN AN
UNSUSTAINABLE INDUSTRY
WITH A DEADLY IMPACT ON
THE ENVIRONMENT.

Inspired by how fashion design can be used as
a creative solution, Aus sustainably designs and
produces pieces under the name 'Trash to Trend'.
She makes clothing and costumes for fashion, theatre
and film, injecting new life into discarded garments,
production leftovers and other cast-off material,
repurposing both pre- and post-consumer waste.
Working with recycled materials in her theatre and
film work, Aus has made costumes for a string of
critically acclaimed theatrical productions in Estonia
and Russia, which have toured globally and won
multiple awards. Aus's own collection features simple,
clean and wearable designs produced from minutely
patchworked textiles. Fabric, colour and textural
combinations are sophisticated and tasteful, often
monochromatic and exquisitely finished with an
eye for detail.

All about finding environmental solutions for the
fashion industry, 'Trash to Trend' is a collection,
a concept and a digital platform – the outgrowth of
Aus's doctoral research and experimentation with
upcycling in fashion and theatre-costume design.
To share upcycling ideas and experience, Aus created
the platform with one simple aim in mind: to extend
the life of materials by reinserting them back into
the production cycle. Using local resources, upcycled
designs have minimal environmental impact and

THE PREDOMINATELY
BLACK COLLECTION (LEFT)
IS REMADE FROM WORN
AND DISCARDED DENIM
JEANS PIECED TOGETHER
WITH RECYCLED TROUSER
FABRIC AND VELVET.

a transparent production cycle. The interactive virtual platform allows direct communication between waste generators, designers and clients, to enable the sharing of ideas and knowledge, and even to sell their products. Consumers, DIY'ers, designers and manufacturers are all able to participate by taking materials of little or no value and adding worth through labour, creativity and design.

The website is designed to aid three distinct tiers: individuals, independent designers and mass producers. DIY'ers and custom designers are able to access a waste-mapping database of relevant and local textile waste streams by both type and quantity. This enables them to create with minimal environmental impact. The website also allows for a more professional approach through access to designer patterns. Video tutorials, workshops and courses are posted on the site for anyone wanting to learn new techniques for upcycling waste into beautiful creations, and feature solutions for individual one-off pieces, small-scale manufacture and mass production. Upcycled products, womenswear and accessories can also be sold and marketed on the site – all in the spirit of spreading waste reuse far and wide.

THE DENIM COLLECTION WAS
PRODUCED ENTIRELY FROM
SCRAPS OF BLACK AND INDIGO
DENIM IN A VARIETY OF
SHADES, DECONSTRUCTED AND
PATCHED TOGETHER AGAIN.

SANHISTOIRE

SANHISTOIRE MELDS HISTORY, AUTHENTICITY AND HEALTH TO CREATE AN ECLECTIC JEWELRY COLLECTION DESIGNED AROUND HISTORIC PHARMACEUTICAL PACKAGING AND LABELLING.

Ransacking the cellar of her family's pharmacy, Silvia Monti Santini discovered an old wooden first-aid box from an English military camp, hidden under thick layers of dust. Driven by curiosity and trepidation, Santini opened her find to reveal layers of history and a multitude of stories: each item within was adorned with exquisite, vintage labelling and wonderfully dated, faded tags. The graphically decorated medicine boxes, with their galenic and alembic formulations, were part of the history of the Santini family pharmacy, and offered a window on to the past. The desire to bring the pharmacy's stories back to life fuelled Silvia Monti Santini's imagination and creativity, and led to the development of the exclusive Sanhistoire collection of bijoux and accessories.

The name Sanhistoire is a combination of the French words *santé*, meaning health, and *histoire* (history). Each piece in the collection is produced in limited editions, and incorporates an original 1920s tag from the family pharmacy, recycling genuine historic pharmaceutical labelling for this eclectic, retro brand. The collection of jewels and baubles is complemented by a range of bold bags and purses, emblazoned with montages of labelling graphics, retro baby-product pictures and skull-and-crossbones.

DESIGNERS WORKING WITH UNUSED MATERIALS

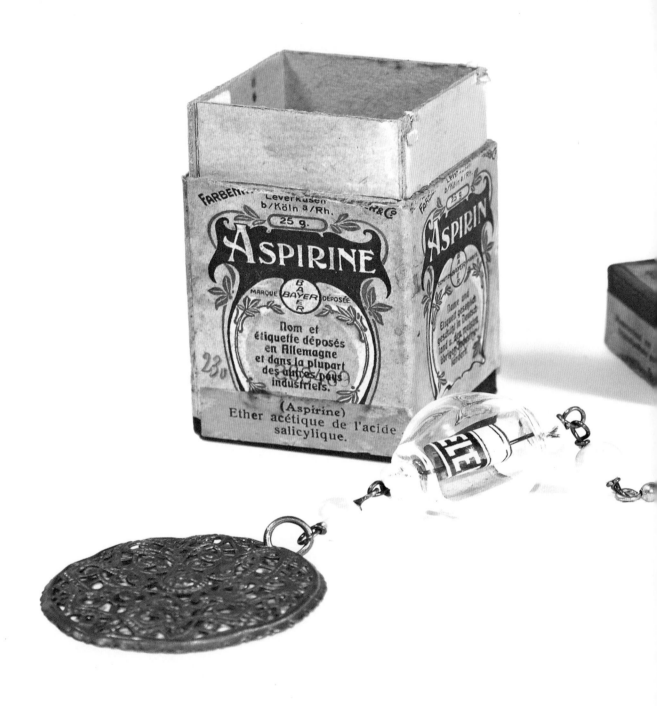

DESIGNERS WORKING WITH UNUSED MATERIALS

AUTHENTIC VINTAGE ITALIAN
PHARMACEUTICAL LABELS
FROM THE 1920S ADORN EACH
PIECE IN THE COLLECTION.

The array of tins and wooden and cardboard boxes – utilitarian packaging in pharmaceutical white and dried-blood red, fading and marked with age spots, mould and rust – would delight any true flea market aficionado. Antique French script and Art Nouveau graphics are punctuated with vintage skull-and-crossbones, and prescription-style forms and labels. Each box holds a treasure trove of adornments, bearing scrolled labels encapsulated within baubles, chain-linked, framed graphics and enamelled red crosses. Pieces of jewelry made from natural horn and wood sport vintage 1920s tags from the basement find. Double-finger rings carry unadulterated medicinal labelling, simply framed, while chain-linked baubles dangle remedy names and descriptions such as Frizioni, Gargarismo and Acido Borico. Intrinsically Italian through its heritage and family pride, the brand is available across that country.

STEINWIDDER

AUSTRIAN LABEL STEINWIDDER
WORKS WITH PRE- AND
POST-CONSUMER WASTE
TO PRODUCE AN AUTHENTIC,
UNIQUE AND CREATIVE
WOMENSWEAR COLLECTION.

The biggest part of this collection is produced from a very unique source: damaged pre-consumer factory-made socks. Working directly with a sock manufacturer, the socks are reconfigured by Steinwidder into sloppy off-the-shoulder sweater dresses, leggings, slouchy trousers and hooded tops. The collection has a fittingly rebellious, grunge aesthetic, with a bit of rocker chic thrown in for good measure. The monochromatic designs rely heavily on textural and shape differences. The shape of the patchworked socks varies in size, making for a complex and detailed base fabric. The socks are interlocked, like an oversize jigsaw puzzle, to make a continuous piece of fabric, then styled into individual designs. Designer Anita Steinwidder uses her architectural background to transform the socks into stylish designs without the introduction of any other supporting materials, inserts or backing.

The collection has a contemporary and edgy feel, going against the idea of the boring everyday, monochromatic ankle sock. Pieced together, often in tone-on-tone colour combinations, and with

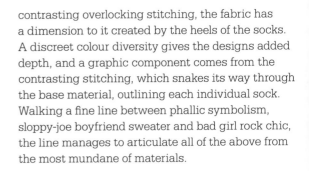

contrasting overlocking stitching, the fabric has a dimension to it created by the heels of the socks. A discreet colour diversity gives the designs added depth, and a graphic component comes from the contrasting stitching, which snakes its way through the base material, outlining each individual sock. Walking a fine line between phallic symbolism, sloppy-joe boyfriend sweater and bad girl rock chic, the line manages to articulate all of the above from the most mundane of materials.

Steinwidder also cuts up discarded and worn T-shirts and sweatshirts, reconfiguring them into new compositions. Within each design, Steinwidder never mixes her source materials: items are either made from sock, T-shirt or sweatshirt. Sourced in Austria, all textiles come from flea markets, factories or social services employment projects that collect worn-out garments, wash and prepare them for resale. Steinwidder uses the rejects that cannot be resold. Working solely with worn-out clothing and overstock, she decided from the beginning that these unwanted leftovers were a rich resource that warranted further processing.

With a particular emphasis on shape, structure and surface, Steinwidder constructs the pieces herself. The 'Shape Series' sock collection incorporates 15 styles as its base, all in a single colour and material and sourced from a German factory. In her small studio space in Vienna, Steinwidder oversees and monitors every step of the process, which involves washing, ironing and sorting into colours. Each design is individually pieced on the mannequin, meaning that each piece is unique and limited in series to the size and scale of the source.

The label on the garment reads:

SW | STEINWIDDER
LIMITED
EDITION
07 *||* 2

THIS PIECE IS PART OF
THE REMADE FASHION SERIES

MADE FROM USED SOCKS
COLLECTED IN AUSTRIA
HANDCRAFTED IN VIENNA
PRODUCTION TIME: 5 HOURS

TRASH-COUTURE CREATES
A COLLECTION OF EVENING
DRESSES AND COCKTAIL
GOWNS USING LEFTOVER
FABRIC FROM EUROPEAN
COUTURE HOUSES.

Established in 2002, its one-of-a-kind designs are hand-coloured, sculpted and sewn in Denmark. Delicate yet audacious designs are at once precious and artistic in expression. True to the concept of couture, Trash-Couture belongs to another world – a world of fantasy and dreams, of aspiration and art, combined with a respect for tradition and craft. Flights of fancy fall somewhere between fairytale heroine and vampire queen, Tim Burton's *Alice in Wonderland* and the style of the female lead in *The Matrix*. The label's greatest fans and collectors are from the parallel worlds of film and music, where they have achieved cult status, outfitting punk divas and innocent angels alike. Trash-Couture enjoys a symbiotic relationship with these worlds in which inspiration and visual image is everything.

Co-owned and managed by Ann Wiberg and Nanna Lowe, Trash-Couture is based between Paris and Copenhagen. Opening The Ballroom salon in the centre of Copenhagen, the brand follows the tradition of a couturier's atelier. Trash-Couture produces couture-quality evening wear and bridal gowns at more accessible price points, thereby bringing these pieces to a much wider audience than the rarified couture circles. With more than 20 years experience as a couture designer, Wiberg has successfully challenged the most exclusive market in the industry, bringing her visionary designs to anyone with an eye for beauty.

Presented twice a year at the Prêt-à-Porter in Paris, Trash-Couture's designs marry structure, in the form of complex corsetry and underpinning, with diaphanous chiffon and silk overlays. Designs centre on luxurious fabrics, including feathers, lace, tulle, fine embroidery, opulent beading and delicate silk flowers. They flutter somewhere between the ballet costumes for *A Midsummer Night's Dream* and those for the film *Black Swan*. Wiberg's legendary development of the stretch bustier, which underpins many of her ethereal designs, flatters the female form but fits a multitude of body types. Trash-Couture's designs can all be customized, made shorter or longer, with or without sleeves, or with colour changes or details removed or expanded.

TRASH-COUTURE

RENOWNED FOR ITS IMAGINATIVE USE OF RECYCLED COUTURE FABRICS AND VINTAGE LACE, TRASH-COUTURE IS A PIONEER IN SUSTAINABLE HIGH-END FASHION.

DESIGNERS WORKING WITH UNUSED MATERIALS

Working with recycled materials allows Trash-Couture to help reduce landfill, while working to order allows the label to minimize over-production, and exert full control over working conditions and workers' rights. Introducing ethical fashion to the world's top fashion boutiques has fed the designers' aspiration of making a difference in the world. Their fashion shows are poetic and mesmerizing, incorporating dancers, ballerinas and mime, bringing their balletic beauty to life through exuberant movement and dance, with just a touch of French theatre. Exhibiting their work worldwide, the brand has ensured that its ethical message has been communicated to a range of collectors and wearers. As pioneers, they have been praised internationally for focusing on 'Sustainable High-End Fashion'.

WASTE AWAY

DESIGNER RUTH HOLLAND'S ACCESSORIES COLLECTION EXPLORES HOW TO COMBINE INDUSTRIAL WASTE MATERIALS AND TRADITIONAL ROPE-MAKING TECHNIQUES.

Transcending functionality, Holland transforms utility and tradition into precious jewelry, reinventing waste material as elaborate, decorative and powerful fashion accessories. She challenges ideas and attitudes about recycling waste by recontextualizing it. She simultaneously investigates the traditional knotting techniques used in the fishing and boating industries. Demonstrating that waste material can be reworked to represent much more than the sum of its parts, Holland's work stands out visually as well as philosophically. She elevates jewelry from purely decorative objects to works of art that push the boundaries of material use. Her jewelry creation involves a thoughtful design process that encompasses an ingenious use of material.

For her Masters thesis, Holland produced 80 highly crafted and ornate neckpieces that harnessed the beauty of decaying synthetic and natural materials weathered by the sea and the elements. Working with electrical waste from industrial and domestic sources, where function is expressed through colour and form, corroded and worn plastic and rotting fishing rope, nets and plastic wires, Holland creates a disparate union that is incredibly striking. The 'Waste Away' collection raises questions about the value of discarded materials that have reached the end of the physical life for which they were intended. Can new meaning be placed on materials through new use? Can they be transformed into beautiful new objects with completely

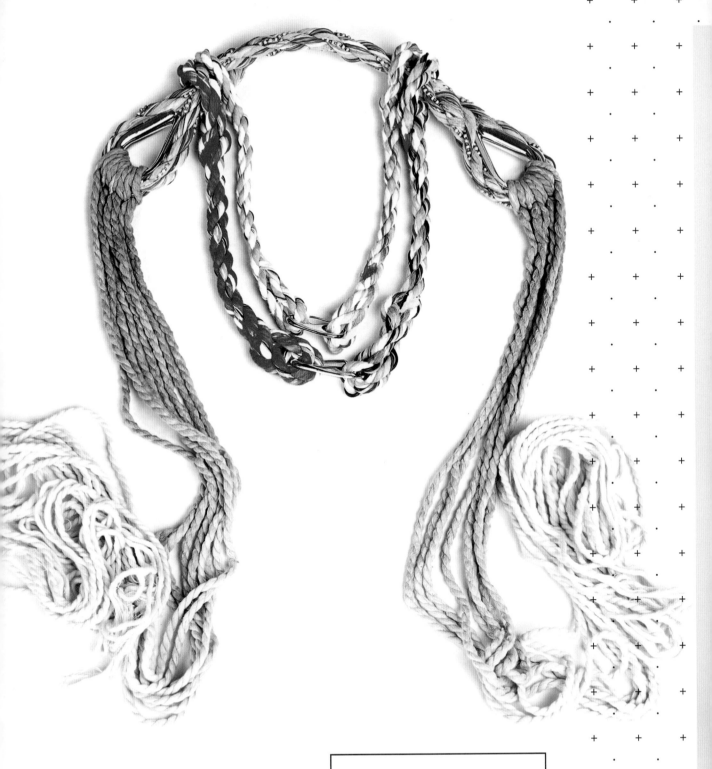

IN MAKING HER FASHION ARTIFACTS,
RUTH HOLLAND TAKES ADVANTAGE
OF THE VIVID COLOUR RANGE FOUND
IN INDUSTRIAL PLASTIC WASTE.

DESIGNERS WORKING WITH UNUSED MATERIALS

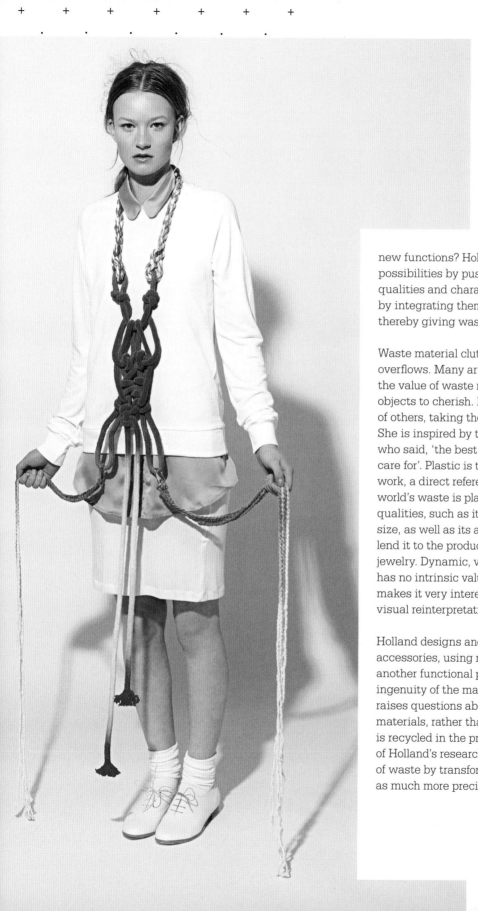

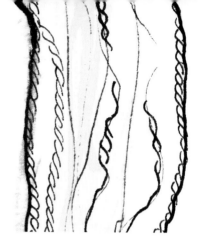

new functions? Holland's thesis aims to show new possibilities by pushing the boundaries of the inherent qualities and characteristics of synthetic materials by integrating them with traditional techniques, thereby giving waste a second life.

Waste material clutters our environment; our landfill overflows. Many artists understand and appreciate the value of waste material, redesigning it into objects to cherish. Holland builds on the approaches of others, taking them a step further in the process. She is inspired by the likes of philosopher Barry Allen, who said, 'the best trash is trash we are prepared to care for'. Plastic is the primary material used in her work, a direct reference to the fact that much of the world's waste is plastic. The material's many inherent qualities, such as its vivid colour range and varying size, as well as its ability to retain its shape and form, lend it to the production of contemporary fashion jewelry. Dynamic, versatile and hard-wearing, plastic has no intrinsic value as a raw material, which also makes it very interesting for artistic, conceptual and visual reinterpretation.

Holland designs and crafts original and thoughtful accessories, using materials originally intended for another functional purpose. Encompassing the ingenuity of the material through her design, Holland raises questions about the transformation of obsolete materials, rather than their disposal. Waste material is recycled in the project, but the primary motivation of Holland's research is to recontextualize the meaning of waste by transforming it into something perceived as much more precious.

RESOURCES

BOOKS

Barbero, Silvia and Brunella Cozzo, *Ecodesign*, Tandem Verlag GmbH, Königswinter, 2009

Bierhals, Christine Anna, *Green Designed: Fashion*, Avedition GmbH, Ludwigsburg, 2008

Black, Sandy, *Eco-Chic: The Fashion Paradox*, Black Dog Publishing, London, 2008

Blanchard, Tamsin, *Green is the New Black: How to Change the World with Style*, Hodder & Stoughton, London, 2007

Braungart, Michael and William McDonough, *Cradle to Cradle: Remaking the Way We Make Things*, North Point Press, New York, 2002

Brown, Sass, *Eco Fashion*, Laurence King Publishing, London, 2010

Clement, Anna Maria and Brian R. Clement, *Killer clothes: how seemingly innocent clothing choices endanger your health ... and how to protect yourself!*, Hippocrates Publications, West Palm Beach, FL, 2011

Cline, Elizabeth L., *Overdressed: The Shockingly High Cost of Cheap Fashion*, Penguin Portfolio, London, 2012

Diekamp, Kirsten and Werner Koch, *Eco Fashion: Top-Labels entdecken die Grüne Mode*, Stiebner Verlag GmbH, Munich, 2010

Finell, Dorothy, *Secrets of Creating a Green Business: Retail, Wholesale, Internet*, CreateSpace Independent Publishing Platform, 2011

Fletcher, Kate, *Sustainable Fashion and Textiles: Design Journeys*, Earthscan, Sterling, 2008

Fletcher, Kate and Lynda Grose, *Fashion & Sustainability: Design for Change*, Laurence King Publishing, London, 2012

Gogerly, Liz, *A Teen Guide to Eco-Fashion*, Raintree, Oxford, 2013

Gregory, Amelia, *Amelia's Compendium of Fashion Illustration*, Amelia's House, London, 2010

Gunn, Douglas, Roy Luckett and Josh Sims, *Vintage Menswear: A Collection from the Vintage Showroom*, Laurence King Publishing, London, 2012

Gwilt, Alison and Timo Rissanen (eds), *Shaping Sustainable Fashion: Changing the way we make and use clothes*, Earthscan, London, 2011

Hanaor, Ziggy (ed.), intr. Lucy Siegle, *Recycle: The Essential Guide*, Black Dog Publishing, London, 2006

Hethorn, Janet and Connie Ulasewicz, *Sustainable Fashion: Why Now?*, Fairchild Books, New York, 2008

Hoffman, Leslie (intr.) and Earth Pledge, *Future Fashion: White Papers*, Earth Pledge Foundation, New York, 2008

Jones, Van, *The Green Collar Economy: How One Solution Can Fix Our Two Biggest Problems*, HarperOne, New York, 2009

Keehn, Dorka, *Eco Amazons: 20 Women who are Transforming the World*, PowerHouse Books, Brooklyn, NY, 2011

Klein, Naomi, *The Shock Doctrine: The Rise of Disaster Capitalism*, Penguin Books, London, 2007

Lee, Matilda, *Eco Chic: The Savvy Shopper's Guide to Ethical Fashion*, Gaia Books, London, 2007

Leonard, Annie, *The Story of Stuff: The Impact of Overconsumption on the Planet, Our Communities, and Our Health – And How We Can Make It Better*, Free Press, New York, 2011 (reprint edn)

Matheson, Christie, *Green Chic: Saving the Earth in Style*, Sourcebooks Inc., Naperville, IL, 2008

Minney, Safia, *By Hand: The Fair Trade Fashion Agenda*, People Tree Ltd, London, 2008

Minney, Safia, *Naked Fashion: The New Sustainable Fashion Revolution*, New Internationalist, Oxford, 2012

Naik, Anita, *The Lazy Girl's Guide to Green Living*, Piatkus Books, London, 2007

Oakes, Summer Rayne, *Style, Naturally: The Savvy Shopping Guide to Sustainable Fashion and Beauty*, Chronicle Books, San Francisco, 2008

Paulins, V. Ann and Julie L. Hillery, *Ethics in the Fashion Industry*, Fairchild Books, New York, 2009

Quinn, Bradley, *Textile Designers at the Cutting Edge*, Laurence King Publishing, London, 2009

Rivoli, Pietra, *The Travels of a T-shirt in the Global Economy: An Economist Examines the Markets, Power, and Politics of World Trade*, John Wiley & Sons, Hoboken, NJ, 2005

Shaw, Jacqueline, *Fashion Africa: A Visual Overview of Contemporary African Fashion*, AFG Publishing, 2011

Siegle, Lucy, *To Die For: Is Fashion Wearing Out the World?*, Fourth Estate, London, 2011

Singer, Ruth, *Sew Eco: Sewing Sustainable and Re-Used Materials*, A&C Black, London, 2011

Snyder, Rachel Louise, *Fugitive Denim: A Moving Story of People and Pants in the Borderless World of Global Trade*, W.W. Norton & Co., London, 2007

Terry, Beth, *Plastic-Free: How I Kicked the Plastic Habit and How You Can Too*, Skyhorse Publishing, New York, 2012

Textile Futures Research Centre, *Material Futures*, UAL: University of the Arts London, 2012

Timmerman, Kelsey, *Where am I Wearing?: A Global Tour to the Countries, Factories, and People that Make Our Clothes*, Wiley, Hoboken, NJ, 2012 (2nd edn)

Vartan, Starre, *The Eco Chick Guide to Life: How to be Fabulously Green*, St Martin's Press, New York, 2008

FILMS, DOCUMENTARIES AND VIDEO-CLIPS

Addicted to Plastic, directed by Ian Connacher, Cryptic Moth Productions and Bullfrog Films, 2008

An Inconvenient Truth, directed by Davis Guggenheim, Paramount Classics and Participant Productions, 2006, www.climatecrisis.net

Blue Gold: World Water Wars, written, directed and produced by Sam Bozzo, Purple Turtle Films, 2008

Fashion's Environmental Impact, by Howard Johnson, BBC News UK video, 21 February 2009, news.bbc.co.uk/1/hi/world/africa/7903079.stm

Fast Fashion from UK to Uganda, by Jack Garland, BBC News UK article and video, 20 February 2009, news.bbc.co.uk/1/hi/uk/7899227.stm

Garbage Island: An Ocean Full of Plastic, Vice Media, 2008

No Impact Man, directed by Laura Gabbert and Justin Schein, Oscilloscope Laboratories and Impact Partners, 2006, www.noimpactman.com

Occupy Love, directed by Velcrow Ripper, produced by Nova Ami, Ian MacKenzie and Velcrow Ripper, Fierce Love Films, 2013

The 11th Hour, directed by Nadia Conners and Leila Conners Petersen, Warner Independent Pictures, 2008

The Age of Stupid, directed and written by Franny Armstrong, Spanner Films, 2009, www.ageofstupid.net

The Corporation, directed by Mark Achbar and Jennifer Abbott, written by Joel Bakan, Big Picture Media Corporation, 2003, www.thecorporation.com

The Cotton Film: Dirty White Gold, directed by Leah Borromeo, Dartmouth Films in association with The Cotton Film Company, projected completion 2013, www.facebook.com/dirtywhitegoldfilm

The Story of Stuff, by Annie Leonard, Free Range Studios, 2008, www.storyofstuff.org

Thread Documentary, directed by Michelle Vey, expected release 2013, threaddocumentary.com

WEBSITES, E-ZINES AND MAGAZINES

Adored Vintage: A blog dedicated to vintage fashion, interiors and weddings, adore-vintage.blogspot.co.uk

Coco Eco Magazine: A digital glossy eco fashion and beauty magazine, www.cocoecomag.com

Curbly: A community website and blog featuring artisans working in various media, including some sustainable design, www.curbly.com

Eco Age: Livia Firth's eco fashion blog, www.eco-age.com

Eco Fashion Talk: Website and blog featuring weekly eco fashion designer overviews and resources, www.ecofashiontalk.com

Eco Fashion World: A guide to all that is ecological in fashion, www.ecofashionworld.com

Ecouterre: Eco fashion, green design and sustainable style, www.ecouterre.com

Fashion Me Green: Style site for the fashion-conscious, www.fashionmegreen.com

Future Fashion Guide: A highly visual eco fashion designer and retailer online guide, www.futurefashionguide.com

Global Cool: A magazine-style site with fun ideas on how to reduce greenhouse gases, www.globalcool.org

Green with Glamour: A style website and blog selling eco-friendly design, www.greenwithglamour.com

Grist: Independent green journalism, www.grist.org

Hand Eye Magazine: Highly visual magazine that focuses on world artisanship, handeyemagazine.com

Hegedus Style: Online eco, ethic and sustainable fashion shop, www.hegedus-style.com

Huffpost Green: The Huffington Post's environmental news, www.huffingtonpost.com/green

Inhabitat: A website and blog tracking sustainable innovations in technology, practices and materials, www.inhabitat.com

Lost in Fiber: An inspirational and visual tumblr site by environmental fibre artist Abigail Doan, lostinfiber.tumblr.com

Magnifeco: Kate Black's eco fashion and sustainable living digital resource, www.magnifeco

The Protein Feed: Daily update on what is new and next in fashion and contemporary culture, prote.in/feed

Rewardrobe: Veronica Crespi's slow style consultancy, www.rewardrobe.eu

See.7 Magazine: Digital magazine for cutting-edge fashion and photography, www.see7mag.com

Six Magazine: UK sustainable fashion and lifestyle magazine, six-magazine.co.uk

Style Will Save Us: A digital magazine for a green lifestyle, www.stylewillsaveus.com

Sublime: A sustainable lifestyle magazine, sublimemagazine.com

The Green Carpet Challenge: Livia Firth's red carpet challenge to wear sustainable fashion, www.vogue.co.uk/person/livia-firth

The Green Guide for Everyday Living: *National Geographic*'s guide to sustainable living, www.thegreenguide.com

The New Consumer: A UK webzine on ethical lifestyles, www.thenewconsumer.com

Treehugger: A webzine promoting mainstream sustainability, www.treehugger.com

INDEX

PICTURE CREDITS

The publisher and author would like to thank the following companies and individuals for permission to reproduce images in this book. In all cases, every effort has been made to credit the copyright holders, but should there be any omissions or errors the publisher would be pleased to insert the appropriate acknowledgement in any subsequent edition of this book. L = left, R = right, T = top, B = bottom, C = centre.

2: The BEA Project – photo by Jeremy Kenyon Lockyer Corbell

6: Alabama Chanin – photos by Robert Rausch, www.gasdesigncenter.com

8: Rachel Freire – photo by Nathan Gallagher

10L: Jeffrey Wang – photo by Liang Su

10R: Raggedy – courtesy of Hayley Tresize

12: Raggedy – photo by Marta F. Andrés, www.martafandres.com

13: Silent People – photo by Elisabetta Scarpini

15: MAYER Peace Collection – photo by Billy and Hells

16–19: photos courtesy of 2ETN

20–23: Artemas Quibble and the Creatures of Mme du Barry; **20BL, 23TR, 23BR:** photos by Koji Ishibashi; **20TL, 21, 23BL:** photos by Weston Wells, hair and make-up by Jenna Kyle, model Keilani at Wilhelmina; **20BR, 23TL:** photos by Ruediger Glatz;

22: photo © Pier Nicola D'Amico

24–27: Atelier Awash; **24T, 25, 26:** photos by Kristyan Geyr Images; **24B, 27:** photos by Davide Grazioli

28–31: CeeBee – photos by Gabriele Balestra, courtesy of Carmen Björnald

32–35: Christopher Raeburn; **32, 35B:** photos courtesy of Christopher Raeburn; **33:** photo by Sam Scott-Hunter; **34, 35T:** photos by Neil Gavin

36–39: Clare Bare; **36, 38R, 39:** photos by Rebekah Schott, hair and make-up by Emily Cheng, model Molly Randall; **37, 38L:** photos courtesy of Clare Herron

40–43: Dalaleo; **40, 41, 42R, 43:** photos courtesy of Dalaleo; **42L:** photos by Valeria Garbarino

44–47: photos courtesy of Denham; **45:** photo by Philip Jintes; **46:** photo by Marijke Aerden

48–51: Jeffrey Wang – photos by Liang Su, artistic and creative direction by Jeffrey Wang, associate creative direction by Caroline Yang at BLANQ, art direction by Wawa Ho and Eddie Teng at BLANQ, hair by Ting Shih at Flux, make-up by Lynn, model Shin at Storm Models, retouching by Chinn, photo assistants Naga Chang and Yang Lin, styling assistant Xiao Bao

52–55: Julia Barbee; **53:** photo by Howard Petrella; **54T:** photo by Julia Comita, hair and make-up by Jodi Vaughn, model Skye Gillian, photo assistance Amanda Jean Fulmer and Kronos; **54L, BR, 55:** photos by Julia Barbee

56–59: photos by Ness Sherry, courtesy of Junky Styling

60–63: photos by Ingo Folie and km/a

64–67: KONDAKIS; **64, 65:** photos by Andre © 2012; **66, 67:** photos by Mia Collis

68–71: Lu Flux; **68, 69:** photos by White Dog Studio, www.whitedogstudio.com; **70, 71L:** photos by James Champion Photography, www.jameschampionphotography.com;

71R: photos courtesy of Lu Flux

72–75: MAYER Peace Collection – photos by Billy and Hells

76–79: MILCH; **76, 77, 78:** photos by Priscilla & Pat; **79:** photo by Mirjana Rukavina, courtesy of MILCH

80–83: courtesy of Nudie Jeans Co.; **80, 81, 83:** photos by Jonas Linell; **82:** photos by Ulf Lundin

84–87: Odette Picaud – photos courtesy of Patrice Elegoet

88–91: Otra; **88, 90L:** photos by Aurele Ferrero, model Anne-Sophie Passalboni; **89T, 90B:** photos by Félix Audette; **89B, 91:** photos courtesy of Otra

92–95: Raggedy; **92:** photo by Aga Tomaszek, photoTOM, hair by Richard Kerr, make-up by Sarah Elizabeth Terry, models Danielle Amber and Jennifer Morgan; **93L:** photo by Aga Tomaszek, photoTOM, hair by Casey Coleman, make-up by Victoria Fox, model Stacey Hughes; **93R:** photos courtesy of Hayley Tresize; **94:** photo by Rafal Tomaszek, photoTOM

96–99: Saisei – photos by Stefano Tedicci

100–103: Schmidt Takahashi; **100L:** photo by Jule-Felice Frommelt, hair and make-up by Katharina Franke at nude-agency, model Anastasia at Satory Model Management; **100T, 103T:** photos by Andreas Kohler; **101, 102B, 103B:** photos by Jule-Felice Frommelt, hair and make-up by Sophia Dietz, models Jessica and Guillaume

104–107: Silent People – photos by Elisabetta Scarpini

108–111: Sylwia Rochala – photos by Justyna Metrak-Radon

112–115: photos courtesy of Tamara Fogle

116–119: The BEA Project – photos by Jeremy Kenyon Lockyer Corbell

120–123: Trashed Couture; **120, 121, 122:** photos by Matt Ford, www.firecrackerfashion.blogspot.com; **123:** photos courtesy of Sara Li-Chou Han, www.saralichouhan.com

124–127: photos courtesy of Ute Decker; **124:** model Tanvi Kant; **125, 127:** photos by Elke Bock

128: Steinwidder – photo by Klaus Fritsch, hair by Thomas Pavlidis, make-up by Richard Schröter, model Jana at Motheragency

131: Hibrida – photo by Pilar Castro Evensen, creative directors Angélica Delgado and Eduardo Sepúlveda, hair and make-up by Coni Montenegro, model Tamie Engler

132–135: Carmina Campus; **132, 133, 134, 135BL:** photos by Alice Tosonotti; **135T:** photo by Mario Grecchi; **135BR:** photo by Aldo Castoldi

136–139: Eva Zingoni; **136L, 139:** photos by Alfredo Salazar; **136R:** photo by Chiara Senatore; **137, 138:** photos by Simon La Salle

140–143: Friends With Benefits; **140:** photo by Dorian Caster at Ray Brown, model Lidia Kochketkova at W Direct, hair by Raphael Portet, make-up by Mathew Nigara at Sally Harlor; **141T:** photos by Matt McAlpin, hair by Orion Boucher, make-up by Angelique Velez, model Hanne Bruning at DNA Models; **141B:** courtesy of Clark Sabbat; **142, 143:** photos by Dorian Caster, hair by Hugh McGuire, make-up by Mathew Nigara, model Chrishell Stubbs at Supreme Debut

144–147: From Somewhere; **144, 145L, TL, 146, 147:** photos by Will Whipple; **145TR:** courtesy of From Somewhere

148–151: Goodone; **148, 149, 150R, 151:** photos by Jessica Bonham, styling by Carley Hague, make-up by Emily Yong; **150BL:** photo courtesy of Nin Castle

152–155: Hibrida – photos by Pilar Castro Evensen; **152, 153, 155L:** hair and make-up by Margarita Nilo, model Sade Hugo; **154:** make-up by Coni Montenegro, model Valentina Dittborn; **155R:** photo courtesy of Angélica Delgado and Eduardo Sepúlveda

156–159: Juana Díaz; **156, 157:** photos by Juan Diego Santa Cruz; **158, 159R:** photos by Alfredo Méndez; **159T:** photo by Paula Labra; **159B:** photo by Francisca Tuca

160–163: photos courtesy of Kerry Howley

164–167: Michelle Lowe-Holder; **164, 165, 166, 167T:** photos by Polly Penrose; **167B:** photo courtesy of Michelle Lowe-Holder

168–171: Paulina Plizga; **168, 169, 171:** photos by Magdalena Luniewska, styling by Sara Milczarek, model Malgosia P at Model Plus; **170:** photos courtesy of Paulina Plizga

172–175: Piece x Piece; **172, 173, 175:** photos by Michelle Blioux, creative director Elizabeth Brunner; **174:** photos courtesy of Elizabeth Brunner

176–179: Rachel Freire; **176, 177, 179:** photos by Nathan Gallagher; **178:** photo by Kate Friend

180–183: R.ds – photos by Monica Bach Nielsen

184–187: Reet Aus; **184, 185, 187R:** photos by Madis Palm; **186, 187L:** photos by Ville Hyvönen

188–191: photos courtesy of Sanhistoire

192–195: Steinwidder – photos by Klaus Fritsch; **192L, CL, CR, 194T, B:** hair and make-up by Karoline Strobl, model Stella Models; **192R, 193, 194C:** styling by Manfred Unger, model Svetlana at Stella Models; **195T, B:** hair by Thomas Pavlidis, make-up by Richard Schröter, model Jana at Motheragency; **195C:** photo courtesy of Anita Steinwidder

196–199: Trash-Couture – photos by Lizette Mikkelsen, www.lizettemikkelsen.com, models Cecilie Madsen, Emilie Rye, Anna Josephine, all at Scoop Models, Denmark

200–203: Waste Away; **200, 201L, 203L:** photos by Philip White, styling by Kieran Kilgallon, hair by David Cashman, make-up by Kate Synott; **201R, 202, 203R:** photos courtesy of Ruth Holland

CONTACTS

2ETN: www.pamelatuohyjewelry.com
Artemas Quibble and the Creatures of Mme du Barry:
   www.artemas-quibble.com
Atelier Awash: www.banuq.com
Carmina Campus: www.carminacampus.com
CeeBee: lnx.ceebee.it
Christopher Raeburn: www.christopherraeburn.co.uk
Clare Bare: www.clarebare.bigcartel.com
Dalaleo: www.dalaleo.it
Denham: www.denhamthejeanmaker.com
Eva Zingoni: www.evazingoni.com
Friends With Benefits: www.friendswithbenefitslifestyle.com
From Somewhere: www.fromsomewhere.co.uk
Goodone: www.goodone.co.uk
Hibrida: www.hibrida.cl
Jeffrey Wang: www.blanqworld.com
Juana Díaz: www.juanadiaz.cl
Julia Barbee: www.juliabarbee.org
Junky Styling: www.junkystyling.co.uk
Kerry Howley: www.kerryhowley.co.uk
km/a: www.kmamode.com
KONDAKIS: www.kondakis.biz
Lu Flux: www.luflux.com
MAYER Peace Collection: www.mayer-berlin.com
MILCH: milch.mur.at
Michelle Lowe-Holder: www.lowe-holder.com
Nudie Jeans: www.nudiejeans.com
Odette Picaud: www.odettepicaud.com
Otra: otra-design.com
Paulina Plizga: www.paulinaplizga.com
Piece x Piece: www.pxp-sf.com
Rachel Freire: www.rachelfreire.com
Raggedy: www.raggedyrags.co.uk
R.ds: www.royalbuddha.dk/category/rds-2/
Reet Aus: www.reetaus.com; sales: www.reuse.ee/trashtotrend
Saisei: www.saisei.eu
Sanhistoire: www.sanhistoire.it
Schmidt Takahashi: www.schmidttakahashi.de
Silent People: www.silentpeople.it
Steinwidder: www.steinwidder.com
Sylwia Rochala: www.sylwiarochala.com;
   sales: www.notjustalabel.com/sylwia_rochala
Tamara Fogle: www.tamarafogle.com
The BEA Project: www.thebeaproject.com
Trash-Couture: www.trash-couture.com
Trashed Couture: www.saralichouhan.com
Ute Decker: www.utedecker.com
Waste Away: www.cargocollective.com/ruthholland

VIDEOS

Christopher Raeburn:
'Remade in Switzerland': vimeo.com/26545234
Fireproof material video: www.dazeddigital.com/video/fashion/7/
scorch-aw12-menswear/728/1
Denham:
www.youtube.com/watch?feature=player_embedded&v=7Ap0mI7xPUA
Jeffrey Wang:
Persona: youtu.be/gHpQ7vg-_yo
The Bea Project:
vimeo.com/25590688
vimeo.com/25382145
vimeo.com/21736033

Author's acknowledgements

I try to tell the stories around our clothing, the stories that connect us back to the materials that clothe our bodies every day. To do that, I rely heavily on the greater eco-fashion community, for having so many worthwhile stories to tell, and for being so willing to share them with me. There are so many designers doing ground-breaking work in avant-garde aesthetics and ecology, and this book is in your honour, in celebration of your work, and to thank you for continuously making the sustainable choices you do. The world of eco fashion is still greatly misunderstood by the vast majority of consumers, as well as the mainstream fashion industry itself. I firmly believe that the combined exposure of the real cost of fast fashion, and the celebration of those making ethical choices every day, will in the long run change the way our industry functions. As more people understand the ramifications of their choices, and the hidden price tag of fast fashion is revealed, I believe we will break long-held habits of consumption and replace them with healthier choices that support the art and design community as well as protect our planet.

There are certain creators whose ongoing contribution and creativity never cease to amaze me, and who serve as a constant inspiration, among them km/a, MAYER Peace Collection, and Natalie Chanin, who also gracefully agreed to write the foreword for my book. Others that inspire and support my work and the eco-fashion community include Abigail Doan of Ecco Eco, Amy Default, Anna Griffin of Coco Eco Magazine, Hand Eye Magazine, NJAL and Above. I am grateful to the universities and foundations that have kindly allowed me to share my passion for cutting-edge eco fashion, through talks, workshops and written submissions, among them Nottingham Trent's Future Factory, T.E.D. at Chelsea College of Art and Design, DUOC UC in Valparaiso and Santiago, Chile, and The Academy of Arts in Sri Lanka. No acknowledgement would be complete without my expression of gratitude to my publisher, Laurence King, my editors Helen Rochester and Felicity Maunder, and my copy-editor Catherine Hooper, w ho has twice now single-handedly worked miracles with my seriously dyslexic misappropriations and terrible grammar! Finally, I give thanks every day for my chosen family: David, Renee, Joshua and Lisa.